RELIGION AND CHANGE
IN EUROPE

Marshall Cavendish Corporation
99 White Plains Road
Tarrytown, NY 10591-9001

Consultants
Professor Charles Ingrao, Purdue University
Professor Ronald J. Ross, University of Wisconsin–Milwaukee

Created by Brown Partworks Ltd
Editor: Timothy Cooke
Associate Editors: Robert Anderson, David Scott-Macnab, Casey Horton
Design: Wilson Design Associates
Picture Research: Jenny Speller, Adrian Bentley
Maps: Bill Lebihan
Index Editor: Kay Ollerenshaw

Library of Congress Cataloging-in-Publication Data

History of the modern world / [editor, Timothy Cooke].
     p. cm.
    Contents: v. 1. Origins of the modern world—v. 2. Religion and change in Europe—v. 3. Old and new worlds—v. 4. The Age of the Enlightenment—
v. 5. Revolution and change—v. 6. The changing balance of power—v. 7. World War I and its consequences—v. 8. World War II and the Cold War—
v. 9. The world today—v. 10. Index
    Includes bibliographical references and index.
    ISBN 0-7614-7147-2 (set).—ISBN 0-7614-7148-0 (v. 1).—ISBN 0-7614-7149-9 (v. 2).—ISBN 0-7614-7150-2 (v. 3).—ISBN 0-7614-7151-0 (v. 4).—
ISBN 0-7614-7152-9 (v. 5).—ISBN 0-7614-7153-7 (v. 6).—ISBN 0-7614-7154-5 (v. 7).—ISBN 0-7614-7155-3 (v. 8).—ISBN 0-7614-7156-1 (v. 9).
ISBN 0-7614-7157-X (v. 10).
    1. World history Juvenile literature. I. Cooke, Timothy, 1961- .
D20.h544 1999
909.08—dc21
                                                    99-14780
                                                       CIP

ISBN 0-7614-7147-2 (set)
ISBN 0-7614-7149-9 (v. 2)

Printed and bound in Italy

07 06 05 04 03 02 01 00 7 6 5 4 3 2 1

History of the
Modern World

Volume 2

Religion and Change in Europe

Marshall Cavendish
New York • London • Toronto • Sydney

Religion and Change in Europe

Protestant iconoclasts destroy religious artifacts during the Reformation, engraving, 1530.

CONTENTS

Introduction

The sixteenth century was a period of upheaval and violence in Europe. The emergence of the Protestant faith, inspired by reformers such as Martin Luther and John Calvin, shattered the unity of western Christendom. As *Religion and Change in Europe* shows, the fracturing of the authority of the Catholic Church coincided with a period of economic and social transformations that made Protestantism attractive to many Europeans. Chapter two shows, however, that the Reformation was no simple conflict between stagnant Catholicism and dynamic Protestantism. The Catholic Church was also reforming its beliefs and practices. Both confessions, however, preserved traditions of discipline and conformity. Superstition also remained a major element of European life, as evidenced in the enthusiastic persecution of witches and others who were considered different.

The emergence of the Protestant faith both profited from and contributed to Europe's ongoing political struggles. As the central chapters of this volume demonstrate, rulers embraced or rejected one faith or another for reasons that were often more political than pious. The Catholic Habsburgs of Austria rose to rule Europe's largest empire from Spain. Europe's other dominant power, France, was riven by the Wars of Religion, as described in chapter five. In England, the Tudors embraced the new Protestant faith and created a strong monarchy based on a buoyant economy and cultural achievement. Chapter nine shows how a change of dynasty, the rise of a radical Parliament, and civil war later led to the establishment of a republic in England. England's cultural and economic flowering was paralleled in the Netherlands, where Protestantism provided the rallying cry for an eighty-year rebellion by the Dutch against their Spanish rulers. Chapter eight shows how Europe divided along religious grounds in the Thirty Years' War, a conflict that brought devastation to large areas of Germany.

If religion lay at the heart of sixteenth-century politics, it also shaped everyday life, art, and intellectual pursuits. The final chapters of the volume show how people sought in religion truths and certainties to compensate for their hard, vulnerable lives. Religion also provided the impetus for some of the great artistic creations of the Baroque age. Both the Catholic and Protestant faiths viewed with suspicion the development of science that threatened to undermine the foundations of the Christian view of the universe. Discoverers such as Galileo fell victim to the condemnation of church leaders who were determined to maintain their primacy in European life.

The Editor

Religious Protest

Challenge to the Catholic Church

On October 31, 1517, the thirty-four-year-old monk Martin Luther nailed a Latin document to the door of a church in Wittenberg in Germany. At the time, this was a common way to initiate debate. In ninety-five theses, or points, Luther protested against corruption in the church. Luther sought only to reform the Catholic Church, but his action would lead to the creation of a new faith, Protestantism. Luther's protest would split Europe, rock the foundations of society, and shape 200 years of political antagonism and military conflict.

The Late Medieval Church

There were many reasons to criticize the church at the start of the sixteenth century. The Catholic Church was the largest, most powerful institution in Europe, and it was in crisis. The papal schism of 1378 to 1417 had weakened its authority. This schism, or split, came about when two popes claimed to lead the church at the same time, each attacking the other and thus undermining the church's claim to spiritual authority. The schism caused fierce debate about whether the leadership of the church should lie with the pope or with councils of church representatives.

In the early sixteenth century, the church was dominated by men such as Alexander

The disaffected monk Martin Luther nails his theses to the door of the church in Wittenberg in this nineteenth-century painting.

Borgia, pope from 1492 to 1503, who bribed his way to the papacy and used his office to amass wealth for himself and power for his family. Catholic priests in many places had a reputation for greed, corruption, and self-indulgence. Church positions were bought and sold rather than earned by holiness or merit.

The church dominated society. It was Europe's largest single landholder. The

151

pope was not only the spiritual head of the Catholic Church but also a relatively powerful territorial prince who governed the Papal States around the city of Rome. Church land needed to be taxed and defended by administrators, lawyers, and military leaders. The growing bureaucracy needed money to fund itself.

In the eyes of many, that money came from abuse of the church's power. People objected particularly to a minor practice with profound implications, the sale of indulgences. These were paper certificates that took the place of the penance and the good works that normally earned a believer's salvation. In effect, it now seemed possible to buy one's way into heaven.

Early Calls for Reform

Luther was not the first person to call for reform. Over a century earlier, men such as John Wycliffe (c. 1330–1384) in England and Jan Hus (c. 1372–1415) in Bohemia had protested against the administration of the church. Wycliffe argued that priests did not possess the power of absolution and that wicked bishops should forfeit their position. Hus followed Wycliffe's teachings. Both men were accused of heresy. As punishment, Wycliffe's bones were dug up after his death and thrown into a river; Hus was burned at the stake in 1415, by order of the council of the Catholic Church.

Both Wycliffe and Hus, however, attracted followers who were dissatisfied with the Catholic Church. In the early sixteenth century, England was still home to small groups of Lollards, as Wycliffe's followers were known, and Hussites still practiced their faith in Bohemia.

Intellectual Background

In the fifteenth century, the intellectual flowering known as the Renaissance encouraged debate on theological questions. Could people earn salvation by their actions, for example, or did it come as a gift from God? Luther himself took a position similar to that of St. Augustine of Hippo (354–430), who believed that people should do good works but that salvation came through God's grace. In many ways, Luther was calling for a return to such principles. He claimed that he wanted to restore the church to its proper beliefs.

The doctrines of the Catholic Church were also challenged by the Christian Humanism of northern Europe (*see 1:59*). Humanists such as the Dutchman Desiderius Erasmus (1466–1536) promoted classical and biblical study as the best way to encourage spiritual growth and morality. Like Luther, the Humanists wanted worshipers to be able to read and reflect on the word of the Bible for themselves.

Luther's Impulse to Reform

The man who brought these currents within Catholicism together was an unlikely reformer. A German miner's son, Martin Luther (1483–1546) was bad-tempered and foul-mouthed. He originally intended to study law. When he got caught in a terrifying storm, however, he made a vow to St. Anne, the patron saint of travelers in distress, to become a monk. He joined a

A contemporary portrait of Martin Luther by Lucas Cranach the Elder. Luther described his own personality as "rough, boisterous, stormy, and altogether warlike."

monastery, against the will of his father, at the age of twenty-two.

In the monastery, Luther spent his days sick with constipation and mentally tortured by feelings of inadequacy. He woke at night in a cold sweat, hearing voices and seeing visions. Then he had a conversion experience. He was struck by the idea of "justification by faith alone." Righteousness, he argued, is not something people can aspire to or earn, but a gift from God alone. Faith is more important for salvation than penance and good works.

Luther became a priest and an influential preacher in the city of Wittenberg in Saxony. On a visit to Rome in 1510, he was appalled by the venality he witnessed. When Luther returned to Wittenberg, where he became a university professor, he began to argue for the reform of the

church. Luther particularly attacked the practice of selling indulgences. When the monk Johann Tetzel visited Saxony in 1517 to sell indulgences to help raise money to rebuild St. Peter's Basilica in Rome, Luther reacted by nailing his theses to the door of the church in Wittenberg.

A key part of Luther's argument was that he denied the right of the pope to forgive people's sins. He later advanced his own interpretation of Christian doctrine, which was based on the belief that a person's relationship with God was a matter of reflection on God's word, the Bible. This view interfered with the established role of the church and its priests to act as intermediaries between people and God. In 1520, Pope Leo X excommunicated Luther for heresy. Luther responded by publicly burning the bull of excommunication.

A present-day view of Wittenberg, the German city where Luther began his movement for reform and where he spent most of his life.

153

Luther found valuable support in Germany. Known then as the Holy Roman Empire, Germany was a collection of individual territories and municipalities held together by nominal allegiance to the Holy Roman emperor, who was elected by seven powerful territorial rulers, or electors (*see 1:19*). Because of the relatively weak position of the emperor in Germany, the pope and the church were relatively influential there. As a result, the pope rather than the emperor was the focus of resentment arising from political tensions between the German states and the Holy Roman Empire.

This was an ideal situation for Luther's beliefs to receive a positive reception. Many people believed that the church needed to be reformed. Princes such as Frederick the Wise, elector of Saxony (1463–1525), also saw Luther's reforms as

Johann Tetzel urges customers to buy the various types of indulgences shown on the board behind him, in a colored lithograph from 1832.

a means of taking a stand themselves against the authority of the emperor and the pope. By encouraging Luther's views, the princes would effectively be asserting their own independence.

Confrontation at Worms

In 1521, Luther was called before Charles V, the Holy Roman emperor, to defend himself at the Diet, or council, of Worms, a town in what is now Germany. Charles was also king of Spain and ruled over large areas of northern Italy (*see 2:183*). Facing the most powerful man in Europe, Luther argued that scripture supported his views. According to tradition, when he finished making his case, he defiantly declared: "Here I stand. I can do no other. God help me; amen." Charles declared Luther a heretic and banned him from the Holy Roman Empire.

The imperial crown of the Holy Roman Empire, studded with diamonds and pearls. With the crown of Spain, it made Charles V the most powerful man in Europe.

Kidnapped

In response, Frederick the Wise, Luther's own prince, kidnapped Luther to protect him from the emperor's men. Held in seclusion in a castle in Wartburg, disguised in everyday clothes, Luther believed himself tormented by the devil. He began translating the Bible into German. It was a vital part of Luther's beliefs that ordinary people should have access to the word of God, as Wycliffe and Hus had preached earlier. The Bible of the Catholic Church was available only in Latin.

Luther returned to Wittenberg, where he spent the rest of his life under the protection of the electors of Saxony. In 1525, he broke his priestly vows to marry Catherine von Bora, a nun who had left her convent. Although he remained tormented by his failure to reform the church, Luther nevertheless lived happily, writing hymns and tracts in favor of reform. His house became a center for the many followers attracted by his beliefs.

A late–eighteenth-century engraving shows Luther defending himself before Emperor Charles V at Worms in 1521.

155

The New Faith Spreads

Frederick's defiance of the emperor and the pope in sheltering Luther reflected the priest's growing influence in his homeland. It also signaled how eager Frederick was to assert his own political authority.

Other German princes joined Frederick in supporting Luther. Some genuinely believed in Luther's message; for others, however, the move was a politically expedient way to increase their power. It was relatively easy for the princes to challenge Charles's power because the emperor was distracted by dangers that seemed far more immediate. Charles's Habsburg empire covered much of Europe. In defending his disparate lands, he found himself facing two main threats: a long struggle against the French Valois dynasty (*see 2:195*) and the threat of invasion by the armies of the Ottoman Turkish empire (*see 1:99*). These threats distracted Charles from the problem of heresy in Germany.

The Schmalkaldic League

The German princes attracted to Luther's teachings combined to claim the right to determine the religion of their own lands. When Charles denied them this right, the princes protested his decision, thus earning the Protestant religion its enduring name. In 1531, the Protestant princes, most of whom came from northern Germany, formed a military alliance against the Catholic emperor. The Schmalkaldic League, named for the town where it was formed, fought against imperial troops for control of some of the German states.

Although Spanish troops from northern Italy defeated the League at Mühlberg in 1547, Charles's efforts to keep his empire united and to defend it from outside challenges were proving too costly. The empire was nearly bankrupt. At the Peace of Augsburg in 1555, Charles conceded the German princes' right to establish Luther's religion in their own lands. Soon afterward, he abdicated his throne.

The Peasant Revolt

While the leaders of German society saw Luther's faith as a way to assert their own power, ordinary Germans were also drawn to Luther's message. Among them were many of Germany's peasant farmers. The early sixteenth century was a time of population growth and inflation (*see 1:29*). Peasants found themselves with more mouths to feed, while at the same time their landlords demanded more labor and higher rents. Many revolts broke out as a result.

The largest revolts came in 1524 and 1525 throughout southern Germany. The rebels looked to Luther for support and inspiration. As Luther taught, they studied the Gospels for God's word. They concluded that nothing in the Bible justified the inequalities of German society. Shocked by the violence and radical aims of the revolt, which was soon crushed, Luther denounced the revolting peasants in harsh terms. The religious reformer was not a radical social revolutionary.

This nineteenth-century statue of a defiant Luther stands in Worms, the German city in which he was declared an outlaw at the diet of 1521.

Luther's Spiritual Appeal

Although the spread of Lutheranism was helped by the political ambitions of the German princes, the faith survived because of its deep spiritual appeal. Among the princes who adopted it, some genuinely believed in the new faith and even risked losing their position by adopting it.

If a prince adopted the faith, his subjects followed. This practice caused relatively little upheaval. Dominated by the Catholic Church on one hand and a distant emperor on the other, many ordinary Germans found Lutheranism attractive. The faith was both reassuringly familiar and refreshingly new. Church services still followed the structure of the Mass, but in German rather than Latin and with more emphasis placed on the sermon as an explanation of the Bible and on the singing of hymns.

Protestant preachers were generally skilled and enthusiastic in their mission to win converts. They had a clear message—that salvation came by faith alone—which seemed a liberating doctrine compared with the Catholic Church's emphasis on penance and good works. The Protestant

A contemporary portrait of Catherine von Bora, the former nun whom Luther married in 1525, painted by Lucas Cranach the Elder.

Luther's cell is carefully preserved in Wartburg Castle. Luther was so convinced that he saw the devil here that he threw his inkpot to drive the demon away.

preachers invited people to reflect on theological questions that had previously been reserved for academic theologians. They wanted all worshipers to take the communion regularly, which previously only priests had been allowed to do. Lutheranism promised to involve people far more actively than did Catholicism in the worship of the church.

Printed Propaganda

Luther's teaching appealed across a range of social and economic classes. For all its wide appeal, however, Protestantism was more successful in towns and cities than in the countryside. One explanation is techno-logical. The reformers exploited the newly invented printing press. The early sixteenth century saw an unprecedented outpouring of printed pamphlets explaining Protestant thinking and denigrating the Catholic Church. Luther himself wrote many such tracts; others were illustrated with crude anti-Catholic caricatures.

The Protestant propaganda campaign specifically targeted urban centers, where it was likely to have the most effect. In towns and cities, people were more likely to be able to read or to find someone who could read to them. Cities also provided the largest ready audiences for the sermons of Protestant preachers.

A pamphlet illustration from 1530, later colored, shows a devil playing a bagpipes in the shape of a Roman Catholic monk's head. Such popular propaganda played an important role in the spread of the Protestant faith.

Vorzeytten pfiff ich hin vnd her
Aus solchen Pfeiffen dicht vnd mer
Vil fabel Treum vnd fanthasey
Ist yetzundt auß vnd gar entzwey
Das ist mir leyd auch schwer vnd ban,
Doch hoff ich es wer auch nit lang
Die weyl die welt so fürwitz ist
Sunderlich dückisch vol arger list.

Protestants and Capitalists

Historians sometimes associate the Reformation with the development of capitalism, the economic system that emerged around the same time. Some historians believe that Protestantism appealed to an emerging merchant class in the cities because of its stress on the value of the individual. The connection, however, is not simple. While some trades linked with a market economy embraced the reforms eagerly, others did not.

Spreading Outside Germany

Trading activity and politics played a part in the spread of Protestantism (*see 1:39*). Germany lay on many of Europe's main

Part of an altarpiece painted in 1847 for the church at Wittenberg by Lucas Cranach shows Luther preaching. His reforms made the sermon one of the most important parts of worship.

This illustrated German hymnbook was published in 1545. Music was important in Protestant worship, as was the use of printed materials.

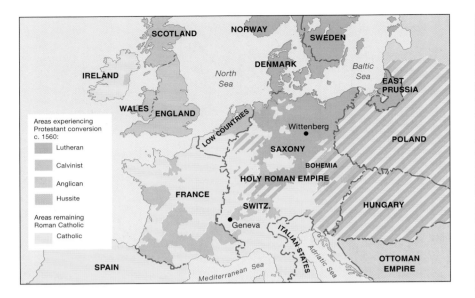

Areas experiencing
Protestant conversion
c. 1560:

- Lutheran
- Calvinist
- Anglican
- Hussite

Areas remaining
Roman Catholic

- Catholic

In the space of half a century, the new Protestant faith in one or another of its forms transformed the religious map of Europe.

trade routes. Merchants carried Lutheran ideas and books north to the Low Countries and Scandinavia and east into Poland. Dutch traders carried the Reformation across the sea to England. Many Europeans had the same grievances as the Germans about the Catholic Church. Some Humanists, though not all of them, also questioned the fundamental claims of the Catholic Church to represent true religion.

As in Germany, however, Protestantism could only take root when backed by the power of princes. In Scandinavia, the competing rulers of the Baltic adopted Lutheranism by 1535, believing it would help consolidate their power. In England, Henry VIII founded the Church of England to help him divorce his first queen, Catherine of Aragon (*see 2:207*). In eastern Europe, though, monarchs were generally too weak to entirely impose or exclude Protestantism. The religion gained followers in Austria, Hungary, Bohemia, Moravia, and Poland. Calvinist missionaries (*see box*) brought much of southern France under Protestant control by 1570; Scotland adopted Calvinism in 1560. Even in Spain and Italy, the heartlands of Catholicism, small pockets of reformers questioned the beliefs of the established church (*see 2:163*).

Other Reformed Faiths

Lutheranism was not the only form of Protestantism. Almost immediately after Luther preached his beliefs, different confessions, or versions, of the reformed faith emerged. In 1523, Huldrych Zwingli (1484–1531) established a form of church government in Zurich in Switzerland. Zwingli had been an army chaplain, and his reforms had a military feel in their discipline. Zwingli, like others to follow, felt that Luther had not gone far enough in reforming the church.

John Calvin and the Spread of Calvinism

John Calvin (1509–1564) was a younger contemporary of Luther, some quarter of a century his junior. As such he belonged to the second generation of Protestant reformers; as an adult he never knew a united church in Europe. Calvin had a unique vision of how God's kingdom on earth should be organized. In Geneva, where he preached from 1541 until his death in 1564, he had the opportunity to put it into practice. For many years, Geneva remained the most important center of Protestant education and training. Calvinism also became the most widespread version of Protestantism.

Calvin, who was French by birth, had been educated in Paris. He trained as a lawyer on the strict command of his father. When his father died, Calvin was free to study his true love, theology. Calvin began to preach the reformed doctrine of Protestantism, but fled France for Switzerland to escape persecution. In 1536, Calvin expressed his version of

An anonymous contemporary portrait of the young John Calvin suggests the discipline and rigor that would mark the church he later established in Geneva.

160

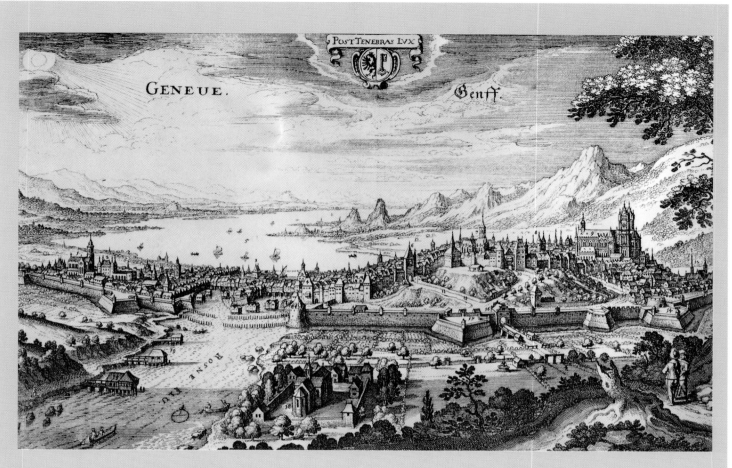
GENEUE.   Genff.

POST TENEBRAS LVX

Protestant theology in the *Institutes of the Christian Religion.* The work gave Protestantism a complete, logical explanation. Calvin dedicated the work to King Francis I of France, whom he tried unsuccessfully to enlist as a protector of the new faith.

In 1541, Calvin was invited to Geneva. The city magistrates had overthrown their traditional ruler, a Catholic bishop-prince, and now asked Calvin to set up a new and independent reformed church.

Despite the chance to put his teaching into practice free from persecution, Calvin went to Geneva reluctantly. He preferred academic reflection to the life of a preacher. Nonetheless, he saw his mission in the city as a duty to God and set out to establish a theocracy, or religious government.

Calvin's theology differed from Luther's in that it was more stern and austere, and much more systematic. Taking Luther's belief in God's grace and the weakness of people to its logical conclusion, Calvin believed in predestination. This meant that everything lay in God's hands and that people had no free will. God alone determined whether people would receive salvation or not. Nothing people did mattered.

The belief in predestination might have led to people living however they wished, if they could not earn salvation by behaving in a certain way. In fact, it led to the opposite: an obsession with living as if one were a member of the elect, or those who would receive salvation. Calvinism became marked by a remarkable moral rigor and discipline. The government in Geneva was one of intense scrutiny and censure of people's private lives. Punishments were harsh. People could be executed for adultery, witchcraft, blasphemy, and heresy.

Calvinism, perhaps because of its rigor, was more evangelical than Lutheranism. It actively expanded and recruited believers. Its influence became particularly strong in Scotland, where John Knox founded the Calvinist Presbyterian Church.

Calvinism was also strong in Calvin's homeland. Calvin recruited young preachers to study at his academy and then sent them back to France to set up churches. As a result, French Protestants (called Huguenots) were almost all Calvinists. This religious minority attracted some support from the nobility. Its influence spread, particularly in the south of the country. Eventually, conflict between Huguenots and French Catholics would lead to the bloody civil wars that split France for nearly forty years from 1562 (*see 2:195*).

A seventeenth-century engraving shows the contemporary walled city of Geneva. The city had grown wealthy by this time, and had become less extreme in its religion.

This seventeenth-century illustration shows the Anabaptist Anneken Hendriks tied to a ladder and about to be tipped into the flames. Hendriks was executed for her faith in the Netherlands the previous century.

Zwingli removed all paintings, statues, and decoration from churches and encouraged civic duty and obedience. From the middle of the century, the equally disciplined Calvinism swept out from Geneva.

More radical groups also emerged. The most notable were the Anabaptists, forerunners in some ways of modern Amish and Mennonites. The Anabaptists rejected infant baptism in favor of allowing adults a personal choice of whether to become baptized (their name, coined by outsiders, means "rebaptizers"). There were numerous groups of Anabaptists. They all shared a distrust of secular government and a refusal to acknowledge any law except what they believed was divine law.

Persecution of Anabaptists

The refusal to acknowledge any political authority made the Anabaptists appealing to people at the bottom of society in Germany, Switzerland, and the Netherlands. Many Protestant and Catholic church leaders persecuted the Anabaptists for their refusal to acknowledge any earthly authority. The most notable incident occurred in the city of Münster in 1534, where an Anabaptist rising was savagely put down.

The Anabaptists received no support from mainstream reformers. Men such as Luther and Zwingli felt they were radical and dangerous. The Anabaptists survived in isolated pockets, however, especially in eastern Europe.

Catholic Reform

A New Vigor

Challenged by the Protestant Reformation in the mid-sixteenth century, the Catholic Church launched a vigorous defense of its faith. This campaign is often called the Counter-Reformation, because it set out directly to combat the success of the new churches. The Counter-Reformation, however, was just one aspect of a more general process of Catholic reform that had started decades earlier. Nor was the Counter-Reformation purely concerned with theology. It also had a strong secular side, as rulers used religion to maintain social discipline in the face of increasing upheaval in the sixteenth and seventeenth centuries.

Ready for Reform

When the German monk Martin Luther sparked the Reformation in 1517, he added his voice to a long list of calls for reform. The Catholic Church was in a state of spiritual and institutional ferment. It had come to resemble a secular power. Increasingly, the popes who superintended the church acted like secular princes. They maintained grandiose courts and became involved in traditionally secular activities, such as art patronage, and in political and factional struggles. Factional struggles also plagued the Curia, the church's chief administrative body, where important Italian families vied for influence.

Abuse and corruption tainted all levels of Catholicism. Officials often held more than one office and cared more about their financial security than the spiritual needs of their congregation. Absenteeism was common, with priests not even living in the areas for which they were supposedly responsible. Such a state of affairs compromised the church's spiritual leadership and raised questions about its role in people's spiritual lives.

Catholic doctrine saw rituals and clergy as providing an indispensable intermediary between worshipers and God. It emphasized participation in the sacraments and church services, sometimes termed the outward forms of religion. The individual

A copy of a contemporary illustration shows the Catholic hierarchy at the Council of Trent. Although much of the council's work was done by committees, all proposals had to be voted on by the general council.

Bildnis des heiligen Merterers
Johannis Huss / Zu Costnitz verbrandt / im Jar
M. CCCC. xv.

Im vierzehnhundert vñ zwelfftē jar / Vor ein Ketzer man mich verdampt /
Nach vnsers Herrn geburt nim war. Vnd wart erbermlich dar verbrand.
Do ich Johañ Hus offenbar / Klar. Doch lebe ich ewig in Gott /
Zu Prag Gottes Wort lert rein vnd Der mich erlöst aus aller not.
Befiehl solchs nicht dem AntiChrist / Ein Ganß brädt ir / sagt ich in dar /
Dem Babst zu Rõ / durch arge list. Vbr hundert Jar / nemet wol war.
Mich kegan Costnitz citiren thet / Wird komē ein schneeweisser Schwã /
Vom Keiser Sigmund gleit ich het. Denselbn werd ir vngbraten lan.
Doch mir solchs nicht gehalté ward /
Vorm Babst ward ich anklaget hart

A ji   Bildnis

A fifteenth-century book
illustration shows Jan Hus,
whose mystical faith and
anti-German sentiment
still attracted followers in
Bohemia a century after his
execution for heresy.

Elaborately enameled and
gilded with silver, this cross
was made to top a bishop's
staff in the fourteenth century.
The Catholic Church, one of
the richest institutions in
Europe, used gold, silver, and
other valuable materials to
proclaim its grandeur.

could find salvation only through participation with priests in these rituals. Now, however, the Church no longer seemed to offer a reliable way to salvation.

Early Attempts at Reform

Calls for reform from within the church became acute as early as 1378, when the unquestioned authority of the church disappeared in the so-called Western Schism. Political wrangling between France and the Italian states, and among the cardinals who ran the church, resulted in the simultaneous reign of two popes. One was based in Rome, the other in Avignon, southern France. Each pope excommunicated the other, or threw him out of the church. The church, whose authority was based on its claim to be the one true faith, recealed itself as deeply divided. The schism created a crisis of faith across Europe.

Partly in response to the schism, the Bohemian reformer Jan Hus preached the rejection of the institutional church, headed by the pope, in favor of a true church that answered to God alone. Similar arguments had already been put forward in England by John Wycliffe. Hus attracted many followers dissatisfied with Catholicism.

Hus argued his case before the Catholic hierarchy at the Council of Constance. The council of churchmen, held from 1414 to 1418, recognized the need to reform the church. It ended the schism in favor of the papacy in Rome and called for reform of the papacy and the Curia. Hus's rejection of the church went too far for the council, however. The cardinals tried him for heresy and had him executed in 1415.

Later councils also called for reform of the Church "in its head and members," meaning from the papacy down. On the very eve of the Reformation, the Fifth Lateran Council condemned the Curia's abuse of its powers of taxation.

Spiritual Crisis
The crisis in the church did not arise only from abuses and corruption. Catholic doctrine grew increasingly out of step with the spiritual needs of its followers as Europe witnessed a growing interest in piety and spirituality, partly as a response to the Black Death that had swept the continent in the fourteenth century. In 1441, *The Imitation of Christ*, a religious manual said to be by Thomas à Kempis, became one of the most popular of all Christian books after the Bible itself. The book delved beneath the surface of Catholicism's rituals to show the inner meaning of the Bible, a new idea at the time.

The Brotherhoods
In Italy, the new spirituality found its expression in many small religious confraternities, or brotherhoods, which emerged to answer people's spiritual needs.

Most notable among these groups was a Roman brotherhood of monks and lay people usually called the Oratory of Divine Love, founded early in the sixteenth century. The brotherhood required its members to attend daily mass—rare at the time—and confession and communion each month, to pray frequently, and to visit the sick. Members of the brotherhood later became leading influences on Catholic reform, which also stressed the importance of leading a pious life.

Humanism
The church came under threat from growing skepticism about some of Catholicism's basic teachings. The Humanists of northern Europe, of whom the most famous was Desiderius Erasmus of Rotterdam (1466–1536), used techniques of close textual examination—acquired from the study of ancient Greek and Roman sources—to interpret the Bible (*see 1:59*). Erasmus believed that the Church's teachings were far removed from the original message of Jesus. In his famous social satire, *The Praise of Folly*, he criticized the church, its institutions, and its servants. The Humanists called for reform within the existing structure of the church. They wanted to place more emphasis upon reading the Bible. Erasmus prepared a new Latin edition of the Bible, correcting many errors in the existing Vulgate version.

Reform in Spain
Late in the fifteenth century, the Spanish Church began to react to calls for change. The church in Spain faced several problems. Some Iberian territories remained under Muslim control; the Iberian peninsula included many non-Catholics, particularly Muslims and Jews. Believing that a strong church would help to unify the country, Spain's rulers encouraged religious reform. The 1478 meeting of the council of the Spanish Church at Seville encouraged internal reform.

The council set the pattern for later reform. It bound bishops to live in their dioceses for at least six months a year, to eradicate absenteeism. It emphasized the

A contemporary chronicle shows the symbolic casting out of Pope Benedict XIII from the Council of Constance in 1417. Benedict was the pope in Avignon, whose claim the council rejected in favor of that of the pope in Rome.

165

This crucifix was carved in the Holy Roman Empire in 1514. The Catholic Church believed such images were a vital and powerful way to communicate the Christian message.

A wooden carving depicts Spanish priests forcibly baptizing Muslim prisoners in Granada in 1492. The struggle to throw Islam out of Spain helped create a dynamic Spanish Church.

importance of administering the sacraments and of preaching. The council instituted programs for building churches, seminaries for future priests, and houses for converts and orphans. The reforms left the Spanish Church well prepared to face the religious turmoil of the sixteenth century.

Old and New Orders

Both Italy and Spain witnessed a significant Catholic spiritual revival in the late fifteenth century. New religious orders arose, while existing orders instituted reforms. The mendicant, or begging, orders, such as the Franciscans, attracted many recruits eager to live according to their ideals of poverty. Some Franciscans wanted to adopt such strict poverty that monks could not even own communal belongings.

The Capuchins emerged from the Franciscans. Led by Matteo da Bascio, who modeled his life on that of Saint Francis of Assisi, the Capuchins—named for their characteristic pointed hood, or *cappuccio*—gained considerable popular support. They lived highly austere lives, tended to the sick during epidemics, walked barefoot, fasted, and preached. The Capuchins later did missionary work among non-Catholics such as the Protestants of Switzerland and France. They also played an active role in Catholic expansion to the east, particularly in Poland.

Reform also influenced female orders. The most notable case was the Carmelite reform initiated by Teresa of Ávila. Dissatisfied with her convent, Teresa created a new convent that would more strictly adhere to the ideal of a humble and ascetic life. Teresa insisted on poverty and complete enclosure, or being separated from the outside world. The nuns became known as discalced, or barefoot, Carmelites.

Many other new orders also emerged, including the Theatines, the Barnabites, and, later, the Society of Jesus (*see 2:170*). Among the new female orders, the Ursulines were the most prominent. They were

Pope Paul III, in a 1543 portrait by the Italian artist Titian. Paul convened the Council of Trent despite the fears of his predecessor that the council would reduce the power of the papacy.

founded by Angela Merici in 1535 to take piety, charity, Christian education, and community work outside the convent.

Pope Paul III (1534–1549)

Although Europe's spiritual revival was underway by the end of the fifteenth century, lasting church reform came only after the Protestant Reformation. Protestantism emphasized close study of the Bible, private prayer, and the ability of the individual to achieve salvation, not by observing sacraments but by faith alone.

The church elected a strong leader to face the new challenges. In October 1534, Alessandro Farnese became pope with the name Paul III. Paul had been raised as a worldly Renaissance nobleman and had a mistress with whom he had children. Once he became a priest in 1519, however, he reformed to live a chaste and priestly life.

Paul III took a number of steps to reform the church. He established the Roman Inquisition—a revived version of a medieval institution—to seek out and punish heresy (*see 2:173*). Stamping out new ideas was only part of the answer, however; it could not succeed alone. The general criticism of the church also had to be addressed. Paul reformed the Curia, appointing cardinals who would support his reforms. Most importantly, Paul also began to work toward calling a church council to discuss internal reform and to address the doctrinal issues raised by the new movements in Germany and Switzerland.

A nineteenth-century painting shows a romanticized view of Saint Teresa of Ávila, who reformed the Carmelite order of nuns.

This silver candlestick, inset with rock crystal, was donated to St. Peter's in Rome in 1582 by an Italian cardinal. During the Counter-Reformation, church leaders were enthusiastic patrons of artists such as the sculptor Antonio Gentili, who created this piece.

Arranging the Council

It took Paul more than ten years to overcome resistance to the general council. Charles V, the Holy Roman emperor, and Francis I, king of France, squabbled about a location for the council. Francis feared that, by addressing the complaints of the Protestants, the council would weaken Protestant opposition within the Holy Roman Empire, thereby increasing Charles's power.

The pope also faced resistance from both sides of the religious divide. Protestants refused to attend, ending any chance of bringing the two sides together. The Catholic clergy also resisted the idea of a council. Some refused to contemplate any reform. Others were reluctant to face a long and uncomfortable journey to participate in the council. Yet despite all the problems and a number of false starts, the council met in 1545 in the town of Trent, in northern Italy.

The Council of Trent (1545–1563)

The council brought together papal delegates, bishops, and the heads of religious orders. It got off to a shaky start. Afraid of upsetting his Protestant subjects, the emperor tried to prevent the council from discussing questions of doctrine. He wanted it to focus only on internal reform. The death of Martin Luther in 1546, meanwhile, did not bring the prospect of an end to the schism any closer. War loomed

between Catholic and Protestant forces. In 1547, an outbreak of disease in Trent saw Paul transfer the council to Bologna, an Italian city to which many deputies refused to travel. The council resumed in Trent only in 1551. It met irregularly for the next twelve years.

The council's resolutions codified the Catholic Church's response to the Reformation. Despite the efforts of Charles V, the delegates responded to the Protestant challenge on two fronts, with internal reforms and with a restatement and clarification of the church's position on doctrinal matters. The council's resolutions gave formal expression to the principles of the Counter-Reformation.

The Council's Resolutions
The council gave the pope increased authority over the church. Bishops also had increased power but had to live in their sees, making absenteeism impossible. The council enforced the enclosure of female religious orders. Nuns who sought to work in the community, such as the Ursulines, had to stop their activities outside the convent.

On doctrinal issues, the council discounted Protestantism's assertion that the Bible should form the exclusive textual authority for Christianity. Works by ancient scholars also had authority. In the face of the Protestant belief in the individual rather than religious ritual, the council stressed the role of the sacraments in individual salvation. Whereas Protestant doctrine argued that faith alone was the means to individual salvation, the council stated that salvation came from both faith and good works, or actions.

Luther and his followers had attacked the accuracy of the Latin translation of the Bible, the Vulgate. The council, however, declared the Vulgate authentic, holy, and the only translation for use in theological debate. Translations of the Bible into other languages were later placed on the Index of Prohibited Books.

Effects of the Council
The Council of Trent tackled many of the abuses that had led to the Reformation. It did not heal the schism between the Protestant and Catholic churches, however. The Protestants themselves refused to take part in any of the discussions. The council itself disregarded or flatly contradicted many of the doctrinal positions adopted by the Protestants and offered little room for compromise. Its clarification of Catholic dogma, in fact, reinforced the differences between the two churches. The clear state-

ment of the principles of Catholicism, however, made it easier to define and defend the church and to identify and persecute those who questioned its beliefs. The Counter-Reformation began in earnest.

Radical Religion
Invigorated by the Council of Trent, the Catholic Church launched a wide-ranging campaign to win back Protestant converts. It enlisted enthusiastic priests, courageous missionaries, and outstanding artists to proclaim the glory of the church (*see 2:255*). In Catholic strongholds such as Spain and Italy, harsh inquisitions sought out heresy and punished it. In England, the brief reign of Mary Tudor saw the violent persecution of Protestants (*see 2:210*).

The vigorous Catholic campaign hardened the split between the two Christian faiths and left no place for toleration. Both

This present-day view shows the church of Santa Maria Maggiore in Trent. The church, built in 1520, was still relatively new when the town became the venue of the Council of Trent in 1545.

This chapel was built in the cave at Manresa, Spain, where Ignatius often spent seven hours a day in prayer during the time he lived as a beggar. Ignatius was declared a saint in 1622.

The Society of Jesus

The most important religious order to emerge during the Catholic revival was the Society of Jesus, or the Jesuits, founded by Ignatius of Loyola. Ignatius (1491–1556) was a nobleman from the Basque region of northern Spain. As a young man, he sought glory on the battlefield, fighting with Spanish forces against the French. In 1521, however, he was badly wounded in the Battle of Pamplona. While recovering, he had no reading material except a life of Christ and a book of lives of the saints. Inspired, Ignatius experienced a spiritual conversion in which he came to see serving God as being like the service of a knight in war.

After a period in which he lived as a beggar and prayed for seven hours a day, Ignatius wrote his influential *Spiritual Exercises*. The book presented a program of meditations, performed over about thirty days, that would lead to personal spiritual perfection.

Ignatius, who soon acquired followers for his dynamic ministry, was inspired by a chapter from the Book of Matthew in which Jesus sent his apostles out into the world to preach the gospel and heal the sick. By now, Ignatius had acquired followers who wore a distinctive uniform. He had also been imprisoned by the Spanish Inquisition but was acquitted of heresy. The Jesuits placed their unconditional loyalty in the pope, who would guide them to wherever preaching was needed.

The Jesuits stressed the importance of education and missionary work. They founded numerous schools and colleges, many of which still exist. They used innovative teaching methods and examined new scientific theories, such as Copernicus's theory that Earth orbited the Sun (*see 2:268*). Jesuit missionaries, meanwhile, proved both brave and flexible in their attempts to spread the faith. Francis Xavier, for example, adopted extreme poverty among the poor pearl fishers of India but used technological novelties to impress the Chinese emperor (*see 4:528*). Such innovations raised opposition from older religious orders. The Jesuits' absolute obedience to the pope, meanwhile, caused secular rulers to distrust them.

sides looked for any way to convert or defeat the other. The radicalization of religion did not only affect Catholics. Protestants had come a long way from Luther's initial tolerance. Luther himself had grown more radical toward his opponents, demanding the banishment of other Christian denominations from the German states if they tried to win converts among Protestants. Even more drastic measures were applied by John Calvin in the Swiss city of Geneva (*see 2:160*).

The Secular Counter-Reformation

The Catholic resurgence also had a political side, sometimes known as the secular Counter-Reformation. The rivalry of Protestant and Catholic often became confused with struggles between countries or between ruled and ruler. In the competition for European domination between the emperor Charles V and Francis I of France, for example, the French king sympathized with the Protestants in the hope that they

The Miracles of Ignatius of Loyola, by the Flemish artist Peter Paul Rubens, shows the saint driving demons from a group of possessed people.

A carving from a Jesuit college in Spain shows Saint Francis Xavier baptizing an Indian convert. Xavier was Ignatius's roommate and one of his earliest followers.

Although the Jesuits helped combat the rise of Protestantism in Europe—they have been called the "shock troops of the Counter-Reformation"—the order was not actually founded to battle with the new movement. Even in places where the Reformation was strong, the Jesuits worked primarily among Catholics rather than seeking to convert Protestants. Jesuits were also active in parts of the world that the effects of the Reformation did not reach. Through their role in education, however, and their effective combination of discipline and flexibility, the order greatly influenced the culture and the character of Catholicism in general.

This page is taken from Ignatius's *Spiritual Exercises*, the work in which he outlined his view of spiritual discipline.

would weaken Charles's power in the German states.

France remained a largely Catholic country, however. The long series of so-called Wars of Religion that swept the country from 1562 to 1598 (*see 2:195*) saw the bloody persecution of the Protestant Huguenots. Despite their name, however, the wars were also a dynastic struggle for political power.

Elsewhere, Protestantism became identified with the growing sense of nationalism that threatened to upset Europe's political arrangement. To the Spanish, in particular, imposing Catholicism became an assertion of their power in the face of challenges from within their vast empire. The Eighty Years' War with the Dutch of the Netherlands (*see 2:215*) saw lines drawn on religious grounds, even though the conflict was as much about political control as about worship. The ferocity of the campaign against the Dutch was equaled only by the ferocity of the campaign against suspected heretics within Spain, led by the notorious Spanish Inquisition.

The End of the Counter-Reformation

By the early seventeenth century, the Catholic Church had virtually reestablished itself. Clerical abuses and corruption had largely died out. New and reformed monastic orders promoted an energetic, practical piety. The Jesuits led a vigorous campaign to establish the Church in the New World, Africa, and the East.

In Europe, many areas lost to the Reformation had been won back for Catholicism. In the heartland of Protestantism in the German states, Bavaria and Austria returned to the Catholic Church. Poland and Bohemia were other major prizes, while the end of the wars in France reestablished Catholic power there, too.

In 1648, the Peace of Westphalia ended the Thirty Years' War (*see 2:225*), whose combatants had divided on largely religious grounds. By the treaty, the Catholic Church acknowledged the legal rights of the Lutheran and Calvinist religions. The Counter-Reformation was effectively over. Religious strife, however, was far from disappearing from the world.

The facade of St. Peter's, Rome, was completed by the architect Carlo Maderna from 1607 to 1614. Maderno's project demonstrated the vigor of the Counter-Reformation Catholic Church.

Dissent and Control

Religious Discipline and Everyday Life

The religious upheaval of the sixteenth century all too often manifested itself in the lives of ordinary people in the form of repression and violence. While scholars and church leaders debated doctrine, Europe's citizens suffered persecution and death because their beliefs differed from those of their rulers or neighbors. It could be dangerous to speak out for one's beliefs or even to be seen as different: the sixteenth century saw the height of a witch craze that killed thousands, mainly women, largely for not fitting in to their communities.

At the root of the persecution lay fear, particularly of Protestantism. The Catholic Church tried to maintain its position by dis-cipline. There was also a political side to persecution. Religion and Europe's monarchies were closely bound, with rulers claiming both a divine right to rule and a moral duty to defend the Catholic faith. Heretics—anyone who believed something other than orthodox Catholic doctrine—were effectively enemies of the state.

A Resurgence of Heresy

In countries such as Italy and, particularly, Spain, fifteenth-century reforms had created a strong, vigorous church, able to face the new challenge (*see 2:163*). To maintain religious control, those countries revived an old institution whose name has come

A contemporary woodcut shows Jews being burned as heretics in the German states in 1493. Jews were a common target for persecution and hostility. France expelled all Jews in 1306, Spain in 1492, and Portugal in 1497 and 1506.

down to us as a byword for persecution and cruelty: the Inquisition.

The Inquisition was an ecclesiastical court established by the papacy to suppress heresies that threatened the Catholic faith. Founded by Pope Gregory IX in 1231, the Inquisition had emerged during another time of crisis, when Christianity faced threats from outside and within. The major external threat was Islam (*see 1:99*). Muslim forces threatened the Christian Byzantine Empire, and much of the Iberian peninsula—Spain and Portugal—also lay in Islamic hands. Between the late eleventh and the thirteenth centuries, Catholic popes launched a series of successive holy wars, or crusades, against the Muslims.

An illuminated manuscript from the fifteenth century shows Pope Gregory IX, in the center, who founded the Inquisition in 1231.

The Cathari

Within Europe, the twelfth century saw the appearance of large-scale heresy. The Cathari—named for the Greek word for "pure"—emerged as an organized church around 1150, concentrated in Italy and southern France. Carried from the Balkans by knights returning from the crusades, Cathar doctrine held that good and evil principles both governed the world. The material world is evil. Catholicism, however, taught that the good principle alone governed the world. The Cathari seemed to threaten the survival of the human race: some argued that all sexual relations should be avoided and that suicide was noble. Papal crusades and the new Inquisition had virtually stamped out the Cathari by the 1270s.

The Waldenses

The Inquisition came to target anyone who represented a threat to the social order, such as witches or diviners. Other major

174

Clad in distinctive white clothes and conical white caps, accused heretics face a court of the Spanish Inquisition in a painting by Francisco de Goya. Late in the eighteenth century, Goya himself faced the Inquisition on charges of heresy.

targets were the Waldenses, a sect begun by a French merchant, Peter Waldo, in the late twelfth century. The Waldenses took vows of poverty and served as traveling preachers. Pope Innocent VIII launched a crusade against them in 1487. Many Waldenses fled to Switzerland and Germany, where they often became Calvinists during the Reformation. In 1535, they funded the publication of the first French Protestant Bible.

The Catholic Church saw Protestantism as an alarming threat, especially as it spread into France and Italy. In 1542, Pope Paul III reinvigorated the medieval Inquisition by establishing the Congregation of the Inquisition, also known as the Roman Inquisition or the Holy Office.

The Inquisition

Operating as a judicial system, with trials and courts, the Inquisition took on the task of identifying heretics and returning them to the Catholic Church. Those who refused

The towering cathedral of Albi, in southern France. Albi was home to the Albigenses, a major sect of the Cathari, who were suppressed during the papal Albigensian Crusade early in the thirteenth century.

An artist's view shows a torture chamber early in the eighteenth century. In the center, a victim is hoisted on a *strappado,* shortly before being dropped nearly to the floor, wrenching his arms from their sockets.

suffered punishment as great as life imprisonment or death.

The inquisitors responsible for seeking out heretics answered only to the papacy, avoiding the influence of local leaders or bishops. They were almost all Dominicans, famed for their rigor and enthusiasm. The inquisitors thought of themselves not only as judges but also as pastors striving to save souls who were heading for damnation. The Dominican inquisitor Bernard Gui, author of a manual on the subject, described the ideal character: "He ought to be diligent and fervent in his zeal for religious truth, the salvation of souls, and the extirpation of heresy."

Courts and Accusations
The inquisitors and their assistants summoned suspected heretics to Inquisition centers. Inquisitors had the power to summon anyone even vaguely suspected of heresy. The word of only two witnesses could secure a conviction.

Often, the first a suspected heretic knew of the charges was when the local priest knocked on his or her door to read the summons to appear before the court. If the suspect failed to appear, he or she was excommunicated. If he or she failed to appear within a year, the inquisitors passed a sentence of heresy. Because there was no right of appeal against the court, many suspected heretics simply fled. They left behind their family, friends, and property to move to an area where they were unknown.

Those suspects who did appear at the center had to take an oath to answer all charges brought against them. Refusing to take the oath or answer questions and lying earned a prison sentence. The inquisitor's goal was a confession of heresy. He would alternately plead with the prisoner and threaten him or her in order to get an ac-

knowledgment of guilt. The prisoner was also urged to prove his or her sincerity by giving the names of other heretics. Thus, the accusations became self-perpetuating, as desperate people gave the names of anyone who might satisfy the court.

Punishing the Heretics

The inquisitors often used torture to extract confessions, though more especially in the medieval Inquisition and in sixteenth-century Spain. Heretics who refused to admit their guilt faced the rack, burning coals, or the *strappado*. The *strappado* was a vertical rack that suspended the prisoner from the ceiling. Hands tied behind his back, he was raised to the ceiling by a rope attached to a pulley or windlass. He was then let drop suddenly until he almost hit the floor. This process was repeated several times, often with weights attached to the prisoner's limbs to increase the pain.

The Inquisition pronounced sentences in public ceremonies attended by representatives of both church and civic authority. The ranking inquisitor preached a short sermon and stated the charges made against the defendants. The kneeling defendants swore off heresy with a hand on a Bible held by the inquisitor.

A wooden torture chair fitted with tiny spikes, used by inquisitors in France. The victim was strapped into the chair until his or her weight made the spikes unbearably painful.

177

This detail from an eighteenth-century print shows a heretic wearing the clothes that symbolize his punishment, in this case death by strangulation followed by burning at the stake.

Chief of the Spanish Inquisition about 1600, the grand inquisitor Cardinal Fernando Niño de Guevara stares out from a portrait painted by the artist El Greco.

The sentences varied greatly. Some penances included scourging, making pilgrimages, or wearing a cross, called the cross of infamy. Inquisitors would impose fines or, more generally, imprisonment. Imprisonment was usually for life but commutations were frequent. Bernard Gui commuted life imprisonment in 139 out of 246 convictions.

Castile in 1479. The new rulers' greatest achievement was to conquer the last parts of Spain still ruled by Muslims. In the newly conquered lands, Muslims still practiced Islam. Spain was also home to a large population of Jews, who again practiced a religion other than Catholicism.

Encouraged by their spiritual adviser, the Dominican monk Tomás de Torquemada,

A witch feeds her familiars in an engraving from 1579. The sixteenth century saw the evolution of the modern image of witches as old women with pets and broomsticks.

Autos-da-Fé

When the inquisitors could not convert a heretic, they turned him or her over to a secular court for execution, usually by burning. The Inquisition itself did not have the authority to execute people. The executions were known as *autos-da-fé*, Portuguese for "acts of faith." In spectacular ceremonies, the condemned were taken to the place of execution—sometimes in large groups—and tied to stakes. After a sermon, the sentence was carried out.

The Spanish Inquisition

In Spain, the different challenges facing the church created a different character of inquisition. The Spanish Inquisition was ruthless and all-powerful. In Spain, the Inquisition proved a powerful political tool for the rulers of a newly unified country, Ferdinand V and Isabella I, to impose unity on their subjects.

The marriage of Ferdinand and Isabella brought together the states of Aragon and

Spain's rulers saw the presence of non-Catholics in their country as a threat to political unity. They asked Pope Sixtus IV to institute an Inquisition in Spain. Torquemada later became the grand inquisitor, effectively making the Spanish Inquisition independent of Rome and placing it in the hands of the Spanish sovereigns. When Sixtus tried to restrain the Inquisition soon after its founding, believing it was too severe, he found it difficult to have any effect.

Tomás de Torquemada (1420–1498)

Torquemada's name has become synonymous with bigotry and cruelty. He became grand inquisitor in 1483 and at once reorganized the Inquisition. He established an all-powerful Supreme Council of the Inquisition to which even priests and bishops were subject. The council also had jurisdiction over local tribunals in Spain's colonies such as Peru and Mexico.

Over the next decade, Torquemada's intransigent personality shaped the Inquisition's campaign to investigate and punish Marranos—the Spanish name for insincerely converted Jews—Moors, apostates, and others. Some 2,000 people died at the stake in Torquemada's campaign. Near the end of his life, he became so zealous in his task that Spain's rulers appointed four junior inquisitors to restrain him.

The Spanish achieved their *Reconquista*, or reconquest, in 1492. In 1501, after revolts and the threat of invasion from Africa, Ferdinand and Isabella ordered all Moors to leave Castile and Granada, unless they would convert to Christianity. The rulers also tried to convert Spain's Jews. In all, around a half million Moors and Jews fled from Spain in the face of persecution.

During the 1520s, the Spanish Inquisition was directed toward people suspected of Protestantism. In 1522, for example, the emperor Charles V introduced the Inquisition to fight Protestantism in the Spanish Netherlands (*see 2:215*). The struggle was not successful, however. The influence of the Inquisition faded; it was finally suppressed in Spain in 1834. The Roman Inquisition, in contrast, still exists, though in a far different form from the past. In 1965, Pope Paul VI renamed it the Congregation for the Doctrine of the Faith.

Witchcraft Mania

One of the most common targets of the sixteenth-century Inquisition was witchcraft. Scholars estimate that witch crazes killed tens of thousands of victims throughout Europe and even in the New World in a period from about 1500 to about 1700. People believed that witches made a pact with the devil, either for power or to harm someone. This pact made witches heretics, because they granted to the devil powers that the church taught lay only with God. A verse in the Bible also supported the campaign against witches, "You shall not permit a sorceress to live." Ordinary people feared witches because they were reputed to do harm to others, making them dangerous neighbors.

Malleus Maleficarum

Catholicism originally denied the existence of witches. As God alone is powerful, witches cannot exist and evidence of them must be fantasy. During the Middle Ages, however, a theory emerged that attributed power to Satan as the equal opponent of God. This dualist heresy convinced more people that evil was active in the world through such means as witchcraft.

In 1484, two Dominican friars, Heinrich Kramer and Jacob Sprenger, persuaded the pope to authorize them to stamp out witchcraft in the German states, thus acknowledging that witchcraft must exist. In 1486, Kramer and Sprenger published *Malleus Maleficarum*, or "Hammer of Witches," a book that helped shape the course of the witch crazes. The book described in detail folk beliefs about witches and their powers. The book also linked witchcraft especially with women, which had not been the case before. It asserted that the origin of witchcraft was "carnal lust," which was insatiable in women. The close connection between witchcraft and women would prove a long-lived popular belief.

The Dominicans argued that suspected witches should be tortured until they confessed. Convicted but unrepentant witches should be executed. *Malleus Maleficarum* was translated into many languages and went through numerous editions in both Catholic and Protestant countries. Both faiths were equally eager to persecute what they saw as the devil's disciples.

Identifying Witches

Malleus Maleficarum contained many popular beliefs about witches. Among them was the idea of the sabbat, a nighttime gathering of witches presided over by the devil himself. Witches were accompanied by familiars, it was said, small demons disguised as animals who helped the witch wreak her harm. Witches stole babies and used their fat as an ointment to make them

This print from 1659 shows a woman recovering after an attack of demonic possession. Many people believed that demons played a very real part in everyday life.

Suspected of practicing witchcraft against her brother-in-law, King Charles VI, the duchess d'Orleans is expelled from Paris in a late-fourteenth-century print. Accusations of witchcraft against prominent members of society were rare and usually involved an element of political, dynastic, or economic rivalry.

fly. On nightly raids, witches flew above the countryside, usually on broomsticks. Witches could be identified by a "witch mark," a mark put on her body by the devil and impervious to pain. Such a spot provided proof that a person was a witch.

Other proofs of witchcraft were equally weak. Sometimes, for example, a woman was thrown into a body of water to test her innocence. If she sank, she was innocent, but if she floated, she was a witch.

Confession and Punishment

Under torture or severe questioning, suspected witches often said what they thought their listeners wanted to hear. Their confessions confirmed the image of witchcraft in the popular imagination. Some of the accused even convinced themselves that they had indeed made a pact with the devil. Others were tricked into confessing. A young boy convicted as a witch and being led out to his death in France protested to the court, "You made me say things I didn't understand."

Torture also elicited the names of other witches. The victim gave some names to satisfy the witch finders, who were paid a fee for each conviction they secured, thus increasing the number of prosecutions. The practice meant that witch hunts grew into great purges. In 1692, a witch craze in

A suspected witch is raised from a pond on a ducking stool in this artist's re-creation of seventeenth-century England.

Salem, Massachusetts, convicted more than thirty people from one community, twenty-two of whom were executed (*see 3:370*).

Fear and the Outcast

The witch crazes thrived in an atmosphere of fear. The Reformation had stripped people of age-old religious certainties and replaced them with doubt and worry. Village life was changing, too, as traditional ties of charity and support gave way to more jealous and resentful ways of thinking. If a cow would not give milk, a man fell down, or an animal died, people suspected a neighbor of witchcraft.

Witch crazes often occurred in isolated rural areas, and their victims usually came from among the most vulnerable members of society: the poor, the mentally ill, and the outcast. Elderly widows, in particular, became common targets. There were various reasons for this. First, such women had no husband to protect them or their reputation. The same lack of a husband seemed to suggest that the women were not controlled and so were a threat to society.

Quite often, such women lived slightly removed from the rest of the community; they often had pets who were easily identified as familiars; they might have a good knowledge of herbs and remedies that seemed like magical potions. Quite often they also had relatively large amounts of property or wealth, making them the targets of other people's resentment and envy.

In some ways, the witch crazes provided a focus for local tension, jealousy, suspicion, and gossip. Accusations rose at times of crisis, such as during wars or in times of food shortages. It was all too easy to accuse someone of witchcraft and all too difficult to defend oneself against the charge.

Women's Role

Not only were women the chief victims of the witch crazes—about four-fifths of convicted witches were female—they were also the chief accusers. Some historians believe that the witch crazes were closely connected with the atmosphere of gossip and accusation commonplace in small, isolated, and humdrum communities. The witch crazes provided a channel for people's frustrations and jealousy.

Although scholars and church leaders wrote about witchcraft and supported the witch crazes, not everyone believed in witches. The sixteenth century saw increasing numbers of judges refuse to accept the hearsay evidence or false confessions on which convictions were based. Eventually, witch trials died out in the early eighteenth century under the skeptical influence of the Age of Enlightenment (*see 4:471*).

Spain and the Habsburg Empire

Charles V and Philip II

In the eleventh century, the Habsburgs were a middling aristocratic family that had its seat in the Aargau, in present-day Switzerland. During the medieval period, however, the family gradually extended its rule throughout Styria and Austria, until, in the late fourteenth century, it was able to lay permanent claim to the throne of the Holy Roman Empire, the loose confederation of mainly German states in central Europe.

The family's fortunes reached their zenith in the sixteenth century, when one Habsburg—the Holy Roman emperor Charles V—ruled directly not only the family's hereditary lands in Austria, Hungary, and Bohemia but also the kingdom of Spain, together with its territories in Europe and the newly discovered Americas. Remarkably, the Habsburgs achieved this territorial expansion not by conquest but by marriage. The family's snowballing success, however, made it many enemies, and the empire ultimately proved unsustainable, at least on such a vast and unwieldy scale.

"Austria Is Destined to Rule the World"

When the Habsburg Frederick III (1415–1493) was elected and crowned Holy Roman emperor in Rome in 1452, it

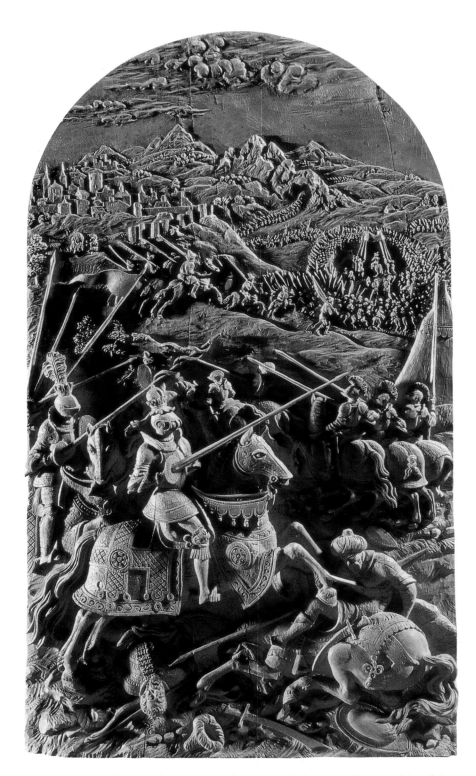

A sixteenth-century wood sculpture depicts the military exploits of the Habsburg emperor Charles V. The Habsburg Empire was the result less of military conquest than of dynastic marriage. As emperor, however, Charles V faced repeated military and political challenges to his power.

already seemed as if the fortunes of the Habsburgs could go no higher. The imperial title combined with the substantial hereditary lands to make the family one of the most prestigious in Europe.

During the Middle Ages, the Holy Roman Empire and the papacy had been the two most powerful institutions in

An early-sixteenth-century dynastic portrait of the family of Emperor Maximilian. The three adults, left to right, are Maximilian, his son, Philip I of Castile, and his wife, Mary of Burgundy. The children are, left to right, Philip's sons, Ferdinand and Charles, and Louis, king of Hungary, who married Philip's daughter Maria. Such paintings served as a kind of political and dynastic "map" of the power structures of Europe.

Europe. At certain times, the empire's territories stretched from present-day eastern France to what is now the Czech Republic, taking in all of Switzerland, Germany, and Austria and parts of northern Italy. By the fifteenth century, however, the empire had lost any real power and was little more than a legal concept. The three hundred or so German principalities that made up the bulk of the imperial territory increasingly asserted their independence from direct control and were held together by what was often only a theoretical allegiance to the emperor. Moreover, the imperial title, at

least in theory, was not hereditary but in the gift of the most powerful of these German princes, the so-called electors. Nevertheless, after Frederick, the imperial title remained with the Habsburg family until the dissolution of the empire in 1806.

Frederick was ambitious. Occasionally, he used the motto *A.E.I.O.U.*—an acronym for the Latin for "Austria is destined to rule the world." He furthered his family's rise, however, less by military prowess than by his matrimonial achievements. The imperial title gave Frederick extra bargaining power when negotiating a marriage for his

856
B. STRIGUEL
El Emperador Maximilianc
y su Familia

This 1519 miniature shows the Augsburg merchant-banker and count Jacob II Fugger (1459–1525), together with his chief accountant, Matthäus Schwarz. The hugely wealthy Fugger dynasty exerted a decisive influence on the political affairs of fifteenth- and sixteenth-century Europe. In 1520, Fugger financed Charles V's campaign for the title of emperor, raising almost two-thirds of the total election expenses.

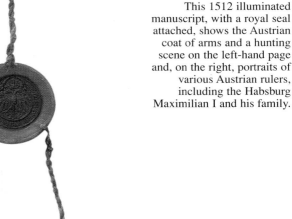

This 1512 illuminated manuscript, with a royal seal attached, shows the Austrian coat of arms and a hunting scene on the left-hand page and, on the right, portraits of various Austrian rulers, including the Habsburg Maximilian I and his family.

lands, Artois, Luxembourg, and Franche-Comté to the Habsburg dominions, although the duchy of Burgundy itself fell into the hands of France.

In 1493, Maximilian succeeded his father as both archduke of Austria and Holy Roman emperor. Maximilian was a visionary prince, full of schemes for foreign conquest and the widening of Habsburg power. He was too poor financially, however, to be successful in any of his military enterprises. Like his father, his chief success proved to be in negotiating a brilliant marriage for his son, Philip (1478–1506). This time, the chosen heiress was Joan, the daughter of Ferdinand II, king of Aragon, and Isabella I, queen of Castile, who brought with her the promise not only of Spain but also the Spanish-held

son, Maximilian (1459–1519). In 1477, by dint of skillful diplomacy, Frederick arranged for Maximilian to marry the daughter and heir of Philip the Bold, the duke of Burgundy. With one stroke, Frederick succeeded in adding the Nether-

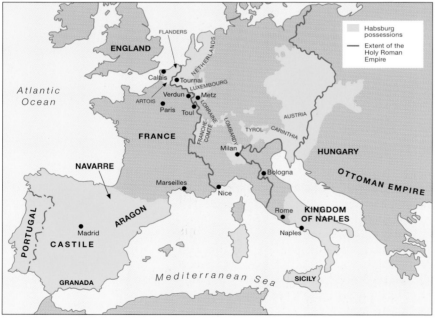

This map of Europe shows the extent of the Habsburg empire during the reign of Charles V.

The Pyrenees mountain chain today provides a natural frontier between France and Spain. In the sixteenth century, however, some territories, such as Navarre, straddled the mountains and were a cause of conflict between these two countries.

The Struggle Over the Succession

Soon after arriving in Spain to live with his wife as heir to the combined thrones of Castile and Aragon, Philip caught fever and died. He left behind him two young sons, Charles (1500–1558) and Ferdinand (1503–1564), and four daughters. In 1516, Charles ascended the the Spanish throne as Charles I and at the same time succeeded to his father's territories in the Netherlands. The death of the emperor Maximilian three years later also left him the head of the Habsburg family and almost certain successor to the imperial title as well.

The prospect of so much power and territory falling into the hands of one man alarmed the other European powers. France, in particular, was terrified of being entirely encircled by a single, antagonistic Habsburg "superpower," controlling the Netherlands to the north, Germany to the

territories of Naples, Sicily, and Sardinia. In addition, this marriage was to bring under Habsburg control the vast territories that Spain was on the point of seizing in the Americas (*see 3:343*). A popular saying of the period remarked on the Habsburg's peaceful acquisition of territory: "Let others wage war; you, happy Austria, marry!"

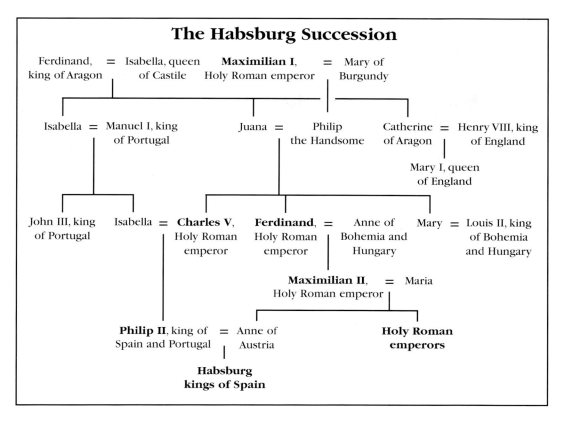

The Habsburg Succession

Ferdinand, king of Aragon = Isabella, queen of Castile

Maximilian I, Holy Roman emperor = Mary of Burgundy

Isabella = Manuel I, king of Portugal

Juana = Philip the Handsome

Catherine of Aragon = Henry VIII, king of England

Mary I, queen of England

John III, king of Portugal

Isabella = **Charles V,** Holy Roman emperor

Ferdinand, Holy Roman emperor = Anne of Bohemia and Hungary

Mary = Louis II, king of Bohemia and Hungary

Maximilian II, Holy Roman emperor = Maria

Philip II, king of Spain and Portugal = Anne of Austria

Holy Roman emperors

Habsburg kings of Spain

The Habsburg succession, showing the marriages that built up the empire and the eventual split between the Spanish Habsburgs and the Austrian Habsburgs, who were also Holy Roman emperors. Bold type indicates Holy Roman emperors and Habsburg kings of Spain.

east, and Spain and Italy to the south. Accordingly, both Frederick the Wise of Saxony (1463–1525) and Francis I of France tried to block Charles's succession to the imperial throne by proposing themselves as alternative candidates.

At first, it seemed that Francis, at least, had a good chance of succeeding. As the election approached, however, it became clear that the German electors would never tolerate the election of a foreigner. Moreover, the powerful Fugger banking house in Augsburg also came out in support of Charles (*see 1:46*), providing the financial resources necessary to put Francis out of the running. In the fall of 1520, Charles traveled to Aachen—the ancient capital of the Holy Roman Empire—and was crowned as Emperor-elect Charles V.

An Unruly Empire

When he became emperor, Charles was just nineteen years old. He was of average height and endowed with the long jaw that was a distinguishing feature of the Habsburg family. He was grave and reserved, but not especially intelligent. Most importantly, he was a fervent, even dogmatic, Catholic. Throughout his forty-year reign as king and slightly shorter reign as emperor, his faith made him an implacable enemy of Protestantism.

The new emperor was faced with a vast and restless empire. During his reign, France and Ottoman Turkey repeatedly threatened

imperial power from the outside, while the rise of Lutheranism undermined it from within. Charles was astute enough to realize that the government of such an unwieldy and troubled empire was beyond the capabilities of one man. Accordingly, he made over the Habsburgs' Austrian lands to his brother, Ferdinand, and, elsewhere in the empire, depended on other members of his family to rule in his stead. Such rulers were often little more than figureheads, however, and Charles was careful to make all the major decisions and appointments himself.

Spain: The Heart of the Empire

Charles paid particular attention to Spain, which would eventually provide him not only with his most loyal troops but also with most of the money for his military campaigns. Initially, however, the Spanish people were resentful of their new king. His arrogant demands for money in order to fund his election campaign, together with his choice of a foreigner, Adrian of Utrecht, to rule as regent in his absence, did not endear him to his new subjects.

In 1520, while Charles was away in Germany, the Castilian town governments, or *comuneros*, rose up in revolt and set up a revolutionary council. With Charles's approval, however, Adrian managed to win the support of the Castilian nobility in suppressing the revolt and executing some 270 of the *comuneros* rebels. Henceforth,

Taken from an illuminated manuscript created in the fifteenth century, this portrait shows Charles V wearing the costume of the Order of the Golden Fleece. Members of the knighthood order were dedicated to the defense of the Catholic Church.

Lutherans and Ottomans

Throughout Charles's reign, both internal unrest and foreign war threatened to tear the Habsburg empire apart. What would eventually prove to be the most devastating menace to imperial, and indeed European, peace had its origins at the very beginning of Charles's reign. In the spring of 1521, Charles met his first imperial diet, or assembly, in the German city of Worms. One issue under discussion was Martin Luther's recent revolt against papal authority and his consequent excommunication (*see 2:151*). At the diet, Luther's patron, the elector of Saxony, Frederick, insisted that his protégé be given a chance to defend his doctrines. When he did so, however, Luther so outraged the emperor that the latter issued an edict in which he declared war on the new creed.

In 1531, the German Lutheran princes responded to Charles's aggressive reaction to Protestantism by forming the Schmalkaldic League. This militant league, which included not only the Lutheran principalities, such as Hesse and Saxony, but also important city-states, such as Hamburg and Hanover, and which claimed to be able to raise an army of some twenty thousand men, was a constant challenge to Habsburg supremacy in Germany.

The Habsburg Empire also faced a threat from the east in the form of the growing power of the Ottoman Empire, which was led by the brilliant soldier and statesman Süleyman I (c. 1494–1566) (*see 1:99*). So successful was Süleyman that in 1529 the Turks were able to lay siege to Vienna itself, and the Viennese were alarmed to see thousands of camels watering at the Danube River. Only appalling weather and the natural advantage always enjoyed by the besieged forced the Ottomans to withdraw and saved the city. Nevertheless, Charles V's brother, Ferdinand, was to spend much of his career holding off the Turks from the Hungarian plains, while Charles's brother-in-law, Louis II, the king of Hungary, lost his life in the campaigns.

The Struggle for Milan

A pressing concern for Charles was the ambitions of the Valois French king, Francis I (1494–1547), who was determined to defend his inheritance against Habsburg power. The tensions between the Habsburg and Valois monarchs erupted first over the duchy of Milan.

In the early sixteenth century, Italy was divided broadly into three parts. The north—apart from the powerful cities of Milan, Venice, and Genoa—fell within the

Charles, though absent from his kingdom for the greater part of his reign, kept stricter control of his Spanish subjects.

Charles did little, however, about creating the administrative or political structures that might have improved his empire's cohesion. There was no common treasury or budget, and his ability to mobilize an imperial army in Germany was dependent on the haphazard support given him by the various princes. Without a sound administrative and economic structure, the Habsburg German–Spanish empire could have little chance of surviving intact the network of political alliances that stood against it. Nevertheless, for several decades Charles strived, through territorial expansion and diplomatic maneuvering, to consolidate his fragmented empire.

Holy Roman Empire; the south, the kingdom of Naples, was part of the Spanish empire; while the area in between was a patchwork of city-states, many of which owed allegiance to the pope in Rome.

Milan's wealth and strategic importance at the gateway of the Italian peninsula made it particularly vulnerable to its neighbors' territorial ambitions. France, especially, was eager to gain a foothold in northern Italy, and from 1499 the city was largely in French hands. For Charles, Milan was a means to link the northern and southern parts of his empire.

In 1521, Habsburg armies attacked France from two sides. In the north, Charles advanced from the Netherlands to seize the city of Tournai, while in the south another Habsburg army took Milan. Not content with merely thwarting French ambitions, however, Charles went on to threaten the French kingdom itself. In 1523, a Spanish army crossed the Pyrenees mountains into southern France, while, simultaneously, an imperial force from Milan laid siege to the port of Marseilles. Francis, however, stood his ground, and the Habsburg assault quickly ran out of steam.

In 1524, the French king seized the initiative and led an army into northern Italy. He succeeded in retaking not only Milan but every other city in Lombardy as well. In response, Charles dispatched an imperial army from Germany. Rather than holding on to Milan, Francis went out to meet the Habsburg force. It was a disastrous move. At the Battle of Pavia, the imperial army defeated the French, took Francis prisoner, and sent him into captivity in Madrid.

Charles did not, however, achieve a great deal by his victory in Lombardy. The 1526 Treaty of Madrid, by which Francis promised, among other things, to restore the duchy of Burgundy to Charles, was not worth the paper it was written on. Francis had no intention of keeping his word, and neither, probably, did Charles expect him to do so. As soon as Francis was released and safely back in France, he repudiated the treaty and once again began to plot against the emperor.

The Sack of Rome

In the absence of the French king, the French regent, Anne of Savoy, had already begun to negotiate an anti-Habsburg alliance among the European powers. Many of them—including some of Charles's former allies—were receptive to the idea. In May 1526, Francis drew the new pope, Clement VII, together with England's Henry VIII and several of Italy's

most powerful cities—Venice, Florence, and Milan—into the League of Cognac.

Charles was enraged. In 1527, with the assistance of his brother Ferdinand, he sent a large German army south across the Alps and on to Rome. There, the Habsburg army sacked the city with great savagery and forced the humiliated pope into flight. Unfortunately for the pious Charles, the sack took on a strong anti-Catholic bent. Among the German soldiers who took part in the sack were many Lutherans, some of whom daubed the walls of the pope's private chapel with anti-Catholic obscenities.

The cathedral tower dominates the Spanish city of Segovia in this modern photograph. The Habsburg monarchs were enthusiastic supporters of the Catholic Church in Spain.

This sixteenth-century ceramic jug is decorated with the double-headed eagle crest of the Holy Roman Empire. Habsburg monarchs from the time of Charles V used the jug and beaker to wash their subjects' feet on Maundy Thursday, a memorial of Christ's last supper.

A nineteenth-century engraving of a much-copied sixteenth-century painting by Dutch artist Antonio More shows Philip II, king of Spain, and Mary I, queen of England. Their brief marriage brought about a temporary alliance between England and Spain.

Madrid, except that the emperor now waived his claim to the duchy of Burgundy. A marriage between Charles's sister Eleonore and Francis sealed the peace.

For almost a decade, there was an uneasy truce between the two rivals. All the while, however, Francis intrigued with Charles's enemies, including the pope and the Turkish sultan Süleyman I. Finally, in 1538, Francis met Charles V at Aigues-Mortes, just outside Nice, and amicably agreed to a ten-year truce. They neatly sidestepped the real issues, such as Milan, however, and instead made a grandiloquent statement about the importance of fighting the true enemies of Catholic Europe, the Ottoman Turks and Protestantism.

This new accord between Habsburg and Valois was short-lived. In 1540, Charles formally invested his son, Philip (1527–1598), with the duchy of Milan. It was a deliberate act of provocation. Inevitably, Francis once again went on the offensive, this time exploiting the alliances that he had nurtured over the previous decade. In 1542, France combined first with the duke of Cleves in an attack on Luxembourg and then with the Turkish fleet in a raid on Nice. His involvement with the Turks, however, largely discredited Francis in the eyes of his European allies.

Charles responded to the renewed French aggression with speed and determination. In 1544, he joined Henry VIII of England in an invasion of France that carried the allies within striking distance of Paris. By now, however, both parties were exhausted and short of money, and in September, they made peace at Crespy.

The Pinnacle of Power

The Truce of Crespy allowed Charles to turn his full attention to Germany and his inevitable showdown with the Schmalkaldic League. Since its foundation in 1531, the League had been a rallying point for Protestant resistance to imperial rule, and Charles was determined to put an end to its influence. In the spring of 1547, Charles acted decisively. Spanish troops crossed the Alps and pursued the League army northward, catching it at Mühlberg in Saxony. There, the battle was brief but furious. The Protestant army, despite its numerical superiority, was defeated and its leaders imprisoned for rebellion.

In the summer of 1547, Charles seemed to be at the height of his power. The Schmalkaldic League was shattered: his rivals for European supremacy, Francis I and Henry VIII, had both died at the begin-

Meanwhile, Francis used the distraction provided by Charles's Roman campaign to lay siege to the port of Naples, Spain's most prized possession in southern Italy. Francis had the support of the Italian maritime power Genoa, whose ships served to blockade Naples from the sea. When, however, Genoa unexpectedly changed sides, the siege collapsed, and Francis was obliged to seek peace with the emperor.

First, however, the emperor brought the pope to heel. By the Treaty of Barcelona of 1529, the pope agreed to show his acceptance of Habsburg preeminence by crowning Charles emperor, which he duly did the following year in the cathedral at Bologna. Later in 1529, Charles also made peace with Francis. The Treaty of Cambrai essentially repeated the terms of the Treaty of

ning of the year, and by June, the Turks, too, were suing for peace. Almost at once, however, the emperor began to run into difficulties. In September, he summoned a diet at Augsburg at which he planned to impose a permanent settlement on the German empire. He failed dismally. The diet's response to his proposal for a unified imperial administration, including a standing army, was lukewarm, and the plan sank under a welter of memoranda.

Charles was no more successful in solving the religious question. Under the so-called Augsburg Interim, he made a handful of very minor concessions to Protestantism. In essence, however, the interim was little more than a restatement of Catholic orthodoxy, and it inevitably failed to appease the empire's committed Protestant population.

The Conspiracy Against the Emperor

It was not long before the German princes were working to free themselves from imperial control. The devious and ambitious elector of Saxony, Maurice, led secret negotiations with the new French king, Henry II. Under the Treaty of Chambord of January 1552, Henry promised the Protestant princes both money and military

Titian's full-length portrait of Philip II, king of Spain, depicts the king as a great military leader. He is shown as if he has only just taken off his helmet, in a brief respite from his struggle to protect Spain and the Catholic Church from the forces that assailed them.

The monastery and palace of El Escorial in Madrid took over twenty years to complete. Philip intended the monastery to be the place where all the Spanish monarchs, starting with his father, the emperor Charles V, could be buried. The building, designed by the Spanish architects Juan de Toledo and Juan de Herrara, was at the time one of the largest in the world, covering some 675 by 528 feet. As well as the monastery, church, and palace, El Escorial contained Philip II's rich library of books and manuscripts.

The modest monastery of San Jeronimo de Juste, in Spain, was where Charles V spent much of his life in retreat after abdicating the throne in 1556.

aid in return for control of three key fortified towns in the border region of Lorraine: Metz, Toul, and Verdun.

In the spring of 1552, Henry marched into Lorraine and Maurice marched south on Innsbruck, where the emperor was holding court. The emperor was helpless. His brother was sulking over Charles's talk of leaving the imperial title to his son Philip, rather than to Ferdinand, as originally planned. Realizing that he faced imminent capture, Charles fled across the Alps into Carinthia. Only then did the penitent Ferdinand rush to his brother's side.

Maurice, however, had no intention of completely humiliating the emperor; his main objective of securing his own position as elector had been achieved. In July 1552, therefore, he offered the emperor peace. At this point, Charles suddenly seemed to recover some of his old fighting spirit. By the autumn of 1552, he was laying siege to the French at Metz and was negotiating a marriage between his son, Philip, and Mary Tudor, who had recently ascended the English throne (*see 2:210*).

Retreat and Abdication

In reality, Charles was exhausted and disheartened. For a long time, he had dreamed of relinquishing his imperial duties and devoting his life to his spiritual salvation. Early in 1555, the emperor took the first step toward his retirement by moving to the relative quiet of Brussels in the Spanish Netherlands and abandoning the day-to-day running of the empire to his brother. The landmark Peace of Augsburg, signed by the German princes in September that year, was thus largely carried out under the auspices of Ferdinand.

In January 1556, the emperor performed the unheard-of act of abdication. Having handed over the Spanish crown to his son and passed the imperial title to his brother, Charles retired to Spain, to a house close to the monastery of San Jeronimo de Juste. There he was able to prepare for his death in peace. He died in September 1558.

Charles's division of the empire into Spanish and Austrian lines was definitive: Ferdinand's male descendants were Holy Roman emperors until 1740, and Philip's were kings of Spain until 1700. Nevertheless, the two branches continued to cooperate politically, as they did, for instance, during the Thirty Years' War (*see 2:225*).

Philip the Wise or Philip the Tyrant?

Protestant propaganda portrayed Philip as a bigot and tyrant, who ruled over a gloomy and secretive court. There is some truth in this image. Philip could certainly behave with single-minded ruthlessness if he needed to. Life at court, too, could be stifling and even dangerous. A contemporary historian wrote of the king that "his smile and his dagger were very close."

There was, however, another side to Philip. The Spanish remember him as *El Prudente,* "the wise," and he was conscientious in matters of state, even excessively so. He was a lover of books and paintings and a lavish patron of the arts. His determination to embrace his Spanish inheritance rather than to adopt the more cosmopolitan style of his father helps explain his lack of popularity among his non-Spanish subjects.

The most important fact about Philip II, though, was his deep love of and support for the Catholic faith. He was an important mover in the Catholic Reformation and a warm admirer of the work of Saint Teresa of Ávila (*see 2:166*). His faith underpinned his politics, both at home and abroad. In 1566, he wrote to the Spanish ambassador in Italy: "You may assure His Holiness [the pope] that rather than suffer the least damage to religion and the service of God, I would lose all my states and a hundred lives, if I had so many."

The administration of Spain and the Spanish empire under Philip II was similar to what it had been under Charles V. Philip benefited, however, from a much larger revenue than had his father. The wealth generated by Spain's colonial exploits was massive, but it is important not to exaggerate its significance (*see 3:388*). At the beginning of his reign, silver from the New World accounted for just 11 percent of total revenue, rising to 20 percent by 1598, but it never exceeded the contribution of the Spanish Catholic Church.

Peace in Western Europe

In the first half of his reign, Philip's concern was to consolidate and defend the Spanish empire. In April 1559, he finally made peace with the French king. By the Treaty of Cateau-Cambresis, France kept Calais and the three imperial towns of Metz, Toul, and Verdun, but finally gave up its claim to the duchy of Milan. Peace with France enabled Philip to concentrate on the

two other major threats to his empire: the westward expansion of Ottoman power and the revolt in the Netherlands.

The Ottomans had taken advantage of Christian disunity in western Europe to strike into Hungary and Austria and also to extend their naval power into the western Mediterranean. Philip's initial attempt to rout Ottoman encroachment on the empire led to a humiliating fiasco. In 1559, he sent forty-seven Spanish galleys to occupy the island of Djerba, which guarded the important Ottoman port of Tripoli. A Turkish fleet dispatched from Constantinople the

The final page from the Peace of Augsburg of 1555 bears the signature of Ferdinand and the royal seals of the Habsburgs. Charles V's withdrawal from political life left his brother to negotiate the landmark treaty.

following year, however, rapidly worsted the Spanish expedition, capturing twenty-seven of the galleys and the six thousand men stationed on the island. Henceforth, Philip was more cautious, biding his time as he rebuilt his navy.

Philip's patience bore fruit. In 1570, the Italian republic of Venice appealed to Pope Pius V and Philip for assistance in countering an Ottoman invasion of the Venetian island of Cyprus, The following year, Philip responded by sending his invigorated fleet against the Ottomans. In October that year, the combined forces of the Spanish and Venetians resoundingly defeated the Turks at Lepanto. The Ottoman navy was virtually wiped out, with 30,000 men either killed or captured.

An Aggressive Foreign Policy

From the late 1570s Philip's foreign policy became increasingly aggressive, even reckless. In 1580, he seized the kingdom of Portugal, its king having died without heir two years previously. Philip's arrogance, not to say his success, deeply worried France and England, who countered by seeking to destabilize the Spanish empire by supporting the revolt in the Netherlands.

Philip gradually became convinced that the Catholic religion in western Europe and Habsburg sovereignty over the Netherlands could be saved only by active intervention against England and France. To this end, he gave support to the ultra-Catholic party in the French Wars of Religion (*see 2:195*) and even claimed the French throne for his daughter. His most daring strike, however, was against England. In 1588, he sent a large fleet—the Armada—of some 130 ships to invade England (*see 2:212*).

All Philip's plans came to nothing. The French people seemed to prefer the prospect of a Protestant king to Spanish interference, while from the start the Armada was dogged by bad weather and inept leadership. Despite these disappointments, Philip's reign was far from being unsuccessful. He had united the Iberian peninsula under imperial rule, staved off Ottoman aggression, and had played a key role in the Catholic Reformation. When Philip died in 1598 at the El Escorial palace, outside Madrid, he left Habsburg Spain still at the very peak of its power.

Windmills such as this one, which still stands on the high, barren plateau of Spain's interior, played an important role in Miguel de Cervantes's *Don Quixote*, written in 1605. In the novel, the crazy knight Don Quixote fights a windmill, believing it to be a giant. Cervantes spent his early life as a soldier. He took part in the naval battle of Lepanto in 1571 and spent five years in Turkish captivity before finally returning to Spain in 1580. Cervantes's writing is a high point of Spain's literary Golden Age, a cultural blossoming that was originally nurtured by the patronage of Philip II.

An illustration from a fifteenth-century French Book of Hours shows the yearly cycle of sowing, planting, hunting, and harvesting. This idyllic vision of rural harmony and abundance was more wish fulfillment than reality: after the 1520s, food was scarce, and the peasantry endured poverty, heavy taxation, and the disruption of war.

The Wars of Religion

Tolerance and Intolerance in Sixteenth-Century France

In the second half of the sixteenth century, a series of nine bloody and devastating civil wars tore apart the kingdom of France. These conflicts were part of what are generally called the Wars of Religion, because the opponents were Catholic on one side and Protestant, or Huguenot, on the other. However, historians have questioned whether the wars sprang primarily from the religious schism of the period. Even at the time, people saw the wars in radically different ways. For one Protestant pastor, the conflict was a religious one: "This war," he wrote, "is like no other ... since we are fighting for freedom of conscience [religion]." The viewpoint of the Venetian ambassador to France of the period could hardly have been more differ-

This painting shows a typical Huguenot church of the sixteenth and seventeenth centuries. This particular church was built in Lyon after the Edict of Nantes in 1598. The circular plan of the church brought the people as close as possible to the pastor, allowing everyone to hear his preaching with ease.

ent: "These wars are born of the wish of the Cardinal of Lorraine to have no equal, and the Admiral [Coligny] … to have no superior." For the ambassador, it appears, the wars were a matter of power politics.

The reality was far more complex than either of these perspectives allows. Even at the beginning of the century, a tangle of social, economic, and political conflicts already threatened the unity and stability of France. These tensions within France were given shape by the religious differences that were splitting much of Europe between the Catholic and Protestant faiths. A succession of weak, indecisive monarchs of the Valois dynasty, meanwhile, meant that France lacked the strong, central leadership that might have been able to keep these powerful forces in check.

Rural and Urban Discontent

In the second half of the fifteenth century and first half of the sixteenth, the population of France, as generally of Europe, rose dramatically. Numbering ten million in about 1450, it had risen to some eighteen million a hundred years later. By the 1520s, agricultural production was unable to sustain such a dramatic population rise. As a con-

sequence, food prices rose sharply. Many landowners were able to protect themselves from economic change, either by imposing additional taxes or undertaking more ruthless estate management. Others, however, were less skillful or less lucky, and their fortunes went into decline. More often than not, this impoverished aristocracy took out its discontent on the monarchy.

While the fortunes of the landowners varied, those of peasants and urban workers were uniform. For them, overpopulation caused inflation, which led to a decline in the standard of living. Some historians suggest that the real value of wages fell by as much as 50 percent during the sixteenth century. Many peasants, forced off the land by greedy landlords, migrated to expanding towns, where work was in short supply. Urban unrest was to be a relatively new and powerful factor in the Wars of Religion.

The economic crisis led to severe social tensions: between king and nobility, between noble and noble, between nobility and peasantry, and between employer and employee. Such resentments underlay sixteenth-century France and were ready to erupt whenever the political order of society was disrupted by controversy.

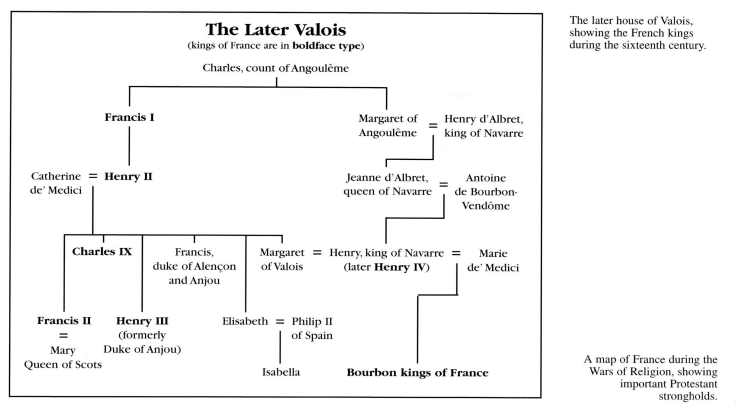

The Later Valois
(kings of France are in **boldface type**)

Charles, count of Angoulême

- **Francis I**
  - Catherine de' Medici = **Henry II**
    - **Charles IX**
    - Francis, duke of Alençon and Anjou
    - Margaret of Valois = Henry, king of Navarre (later **Henry IV**)
      - **Francis II** = Mary Queen of Scots
      - **Henry III** (formerly Duke of Anjou)
      - Elisabeth = Philip II of Spain
        - Isabella
- Margaret of Angoulême = Henry d'Albret, king of Navarre
  - Jeanne d'Albret, queen of Navarre = Antoine de Bourbon-Vendôme
    - Henry, king of Navarre (later **Henry IV**) = Marie de' Medici
      - **Bourbon kings of France**

The later house of Valois, showing the French kings during the sixteenth century.

A map of France during the Wars of Religion, showing important Protestant strongholds.

The Rise of Calvinism

Religion was the principal catalyst of the recurring violence of the sixteenth century. The Protestant Reformation that began in Germany in 1517 spread rapidly to France. There, the French king Francis I (1494–1547) initially gave a cautious welcome to the movement. As the Protestants grew in numbers and became more militant, however, he showed less tolerance.

In the 1530s, a new strain of Protestantism emerged—Calvinism—taking its name and inspiration from the ideas of a young French exile, the lawyer and theologian John Calvin (1509–1564) (*see 2:160*). Calvin left Paris in 1533, fleeing persecution by the French government. Eventually, in 1536, he settled in Geneva, which became the center of the new movement.

In the 1550s, Calvin trained dozens of French Protestant refugees and sent them back to France as pastors and missionaries. Their success was remarkable. By 1561, there were some 2,150 Calvinist congregations worshiping openly in France—a total of two million adherents, representing some 10 percent of the population. These congregations were concentrated in the peripheral provinces of the west, including Brittany; of the north, including Normandy; and, especially, of the south, in such regions as Provence and Languedoc. In France, Calvinists became known as Huguenots—a word that seems to be derived from a medieval German word for "confederate."

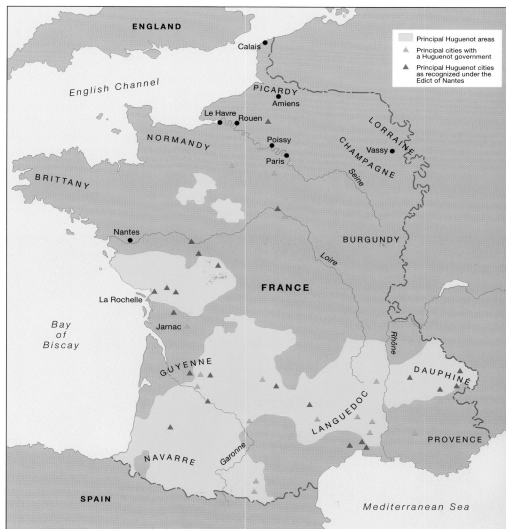

	Principal Huguenot areas
▲	Principal cities with a Huguenot government
▲	Principal Huguenot cities as recognized under the Edict of Nantes

Dating from 1590, this engraving shows Paris standing on the Seine River.

A French sixteenth-century painting shows the three Guise brothers, who led the Catholic faction during the Wars of Religion: (from left to right) Charles, duke of Mayenne; Henry I of Lorraine, duke of Guise; and Louis, cardinal of Lorraine.

Calvinism was particularly popular with the nobility, two-fifths of whom eventually converted. Early converts to Calvinism included a number of influential aristocratic women, though most aristocratic women were not Huguenots. In addition to offering protection and patronage to Calvinist pastors, these women often helped in the conversion of their own families. This happened in the case of the powerful Bourbon and Montmorency families, from which the principal Protestant military leaders were to come.

Sometimes aristocrats converted less out of religious conviction than political or economic opportunism. In the southwest provinces, many of the nobility converted only when their patrons, the Bourbons, did.

Calvinism was also popular among the urban population, especially in the south. There, many walled towns became Calvinist as Huguenots took over local government and banned Catholic services. The peasants were least susceptible to Calvinism. Peasant converts often lived on estates where a Huguenot lord had replaced the local priest with a Calvinist pastor.

"One King, One Faith, One Law"

France lacked a strong government that could keep this volatile situation in check. In the mid-sixteenth century, royal policy was subject to the influence of a power struggle among three great aristocratic dynasties, the Protestant Bourbon and Montmorency and the Catholic Guise. While both Francis and his son Henry II (1519–1559) were able to manage the competing families, their successors could not. After Henry's death, the crown passed successively to three of his four sons, Francis II (1544–1560), Charles IX (1550–1574), and Henry III (1551–1589). Each was more incompetent than the last, and each was dominated by their mother, the formidable half-Italian, half-French aristocrat Catherine de' Medici (1519–1589). Not even

This intricate shield and helmet belonged to Charles IX. The young king, however, was far from warlike. He was mentally unstable and under the influence of his mother, Catherine de' Medici. Charles was haunted by the St. Bartholomew's Day Massacre, which he authorized.

Catherine, however, was able to control the three families, and soon their rivalry broke out into open warfare.

The Conspiracy of Amboise

After Henry II's accidental death in a jousting tournament in 1559, the new king, Francis II, rapidly came under the influence of his uncles, the staunchly Catholic Guise brothers: Henry, duke of Guise, Charles, duke of Mayenne, and Louis, cardinal of Lorraine. The Guise brothers, supported by the papacy and Spain, wanted France to play a leading role in the Counter-Reformation, in alliance with the Habsburgs. Their rising influence was resisted, however, both by Catherine, who had a deep mistrust of Spain and who favored moderation in all religious matters, and the Huguenot nobility, who feared renewed persecution.

In March 1560, two prominent Huguenot leaders, Gaspar de Coligny (1519–1572) and Louis, the Bourbon prince of Condé (1530–1569), attempted to kidnap the king from the royal hunting palace at Amboise. The Guises thwarted the plot, arrested the conspirators, and would have executed them had it not been for the intervention of Catherine, who needed the two Protestant families to keep the Guise family in check.

Civil War Breaks Out

Another political crisis swiftly followed. In December 1560, Francis suddenly died. The new king, Charles IX, was only ten years old and needed a regent, or guardian, to rule on his behalf. Catherine seized the opportunity to stifle the ambitions of the Guise brothers and won the regency for herself. Eager to secure the independence of the French crown and maintain peace in the kingdom, Catherine set about trying to reconcile Catholic and Protestant factions. She convened a colloquy, or meeting, of Catholic and Protestant theologians at Poissy. Even after this ended in disarray, she went ahead with a last-ditch attempt to secure peace and issued the Edict of Saint-Germain, under which Huguenots were granted freedom of worship in the countryside, though not within walled towns.

Catherine's conciliatory policy backfired. Her tolerance of Protestantism alarmed staunch Catholics. The Guise brothers retired from court and began to organize and arm themselves. Religious tensions escalated and finally broke out into full-scale war in March 1562. Catholic extremists under the duke of Guise massacred a group of Huguenots worshiping— illegally—in the town of Vassy. Seventy-four Huguenots died in the massacre.

This detail from a seventeenth-century engraving shows a French musketeer in 1586. Attached to the stock are burning tapers with which to detonate the powder in the musket.

199

This depiction of the events of the St. Bartholomew's Day Massacre by a contemporary Protestant painter was part of the flood of anti-Catholic propaganda that followed the outrage of August 22, 1572. The painter is unsparing in his choice of detail. In the foreground, Protestant men, and women, old and young, are brutally butchered. In the background to the right, the duke of Guise's henchmen throw Coligny headlong out of the window and then cut his head off. To the left, Protestant corpses are carried by the cartload to the Seine.

A sixteenth-century portrait of Gaspard II de Coligny, seigneur de Châtillon and admiral of France. Coligny converted to Protestantism during the 1560s, believing that it provided a sound basis for a just and well-ordered society. He was leader of the Huguenots during the Wars of Religion, until his assassination in the St. Bartholomew's Day Massacre.

Louis, prince of Condé, the Huguenots' military leader, responded by raising his own army. Meanwhile, the Guises, who controlled the royal army and artillery, marched on the king's palace at Fontainebleau. Catherine, with no forces of her own, was obliged to appeal to Condé for help. Rather than face the Catholic forces head on and rescue the king, however, the prince used his army to lead a Protestant revolt. He seized strategically important towns, such as Angers, Tours, Blois, Lyon, and Orléans, the last of which became the Protestant headquarters. Throughout France, Huguenot minorities rose in support of Condé, seizing town governments from Catholic control.

Condé's failure to come to the king's assistance ultimately proved disastrous for the Protestant cause. If he had joined Catherine at Fontainebleau, Condé would have associated the Protestant faith with the survival of the monarchy. Faced with blatant insurrection, Catherine had no

choice but to throw in her lot with the Guises, who henceforth could claim to be defenders of the faith and crown. The result was a decade of escalating civil war, interrupted by brief outbreaks of peace during which Catherine made well-meaning but unsuccessful attempts at reconciliation.

War and Reconciliation

As the decade progressed, it became increasingly clear that the Protestant cause, divided from that of the monarchy, could never hope to win the support of a majority of the French people. Nevertheless, the Huguenot soldiers were a formidable fighting force. Whereas the Catholic troops of Guise were largely mercenaries, the Huguenots fought out of conviction. They often marched into battle singing the Psalms translated by the Protestant French poet Clément Marot.

By the time of the third and fiercest of the civil wars, which began in 1568 and ended in 1570, it seemed as if the Protestant cause

was at an end. The Catholics defeated the Protestants in two major battles in 1569, at Jarnac and Montcontour. The Protestant leader, the prince of Condé, was killed.

At this point, however, Protestant fortunes changed dramatically. Under the charismatic leadership of Coligny—famous for the toothpick he wore permanently in his beard—the Protestants found a new unity of purpose. Coligny's brilliant strategy combined with the exhaustion of the royal troops to bring about a truce, if not outright victory. In August 1570, a peace settlement at Saint-Germain made further concessions to the Protestants and allowed them to keep troops in four towns—including the port of La Rochelle —as a security.

Attack on Coligny

The new peace was superficial. Despite the end of official hostilities, outbreaks of violence between Catholic and Huguenot civilians occurred with increasing frequency throughout France. There was tension, too, at court. With the peace, Coligny began to play an increasing role in court life and politics, winning the affections of the feckless Charles IX. Coligny also showed himself less than tactful with regard to Catherine. Not only was Coligny in favor of what Catherine considered would be a disastrous war with Spain over the Netherlands (*see 2:215*), he also encouraged the enmity between her three much-loved surviving sons, the king and the dukes of Anjou and Alençon.

In August 1572, an assassin shot and wounded Coligny as he left the king's apartments at the Louvre palace. Historians have since debated who was responsible for the attack, usually blaming either Catherine or the Guise family, or both. Whatever the truth of the matter, this attempted assassination led to one of the bloodiest episodes in French history.

The St. Bartholomew's Day Massacre

Charles, persuaded by his mother that a Huguenot revolt was imminent, made a preemptive strike. Circumstances favored the king. The whole of the Protestant leadership was in Paris to celebrate the marriage of the king's sister, Marguerite de Valois, to the Protestant Henry, king of Navarre (1553–1610). The Treaty of Saint-Germain saw the marriage as a seal to the Catholic–Protestant peace. Early in the morning on August 24, St. Bartholomew's Day, the king's guard butchered the bedridden Coligny and almost all of the Protestant leaders. A mob paraded

Coligny's headless body through the streets. Of the Protestant leaders, only Henry of Navarre and another Condé prince survived. Given the choice of death, life imprisonment, or conversion, both eventually chose the last.

The king and Catherine severely underestimated both the extremism of the Guise family and the anti-Protestant feeling of the people of Paris. The murders sparked a massacre of unprecedented proportions. Catholic crowds poured through the streets of Paris, murdering and mutilating Huguenots and dumping their bodies into the Seine. In all, some two or three thousand Protestants died in the capital.

The anti-Protestant frenzy rapidly spread beyond the capital. When it finally subsided in October, another three thousand of France's Huguenots lay dead. Many of the Protestant survivors fled to the western port of La Rochelle, which had long been a Calvinist stronghold. Royal forces under the command of the king's brother Henry, duke of Anjou, laid siege to the city. For several months, the inhabitants of La Rochelle resisted gallantly before they surrendered on relatively generous peace terms. These included the freedom of private worship.

After the Massacre

Catholic Europe, meanwhile, greeted the St. Bartholomew's Day Massacre with joy. In Rome, Pope Gregory XIII held a service of thanksgiving and had a commemorative coin struck, one side of which depicted an angel supervising the murder of Coligny.

For the Protestants, the massacre was a severe blow. Much of their leadership, along with some five thousand or more of the rank and file, lay dead. Many thousands more converted to Catholicism or fled to nearby Protestant countries, such as England. The French Protestant population shrank dramatically. In Rouen, for instance, a Huguenot community that once numbered 16,500 was reduced to 3,000.

In one sense, however, the massacre aided the Protestant cause. In its wake, thousands of Protestant pamphlets appeared justifying popular resistance to royal oppression. One of the most important proponents of resistance was Theodore Beza (1519–1605), who had been a representative at the Colloquy of Poissy. In his 1574 *On the Right of Magistrates over Their Subjects*, Beza argued that subjects were not duty-bound to obey a king who had offended God or Christianity. The weak-willed and arbitrary actions of Charles IX removed any last doubts Protestants may have had about the legitimacy of fighting against a God-ordained king.

The Resumption of Civil War

The massacre brought about a renewed cycle of bloody war and tense peace. Over the next twelve years, Catholic and Protestant armies fought each other bitterly but indecisively. The king, now the erratic Henry III, the former duke of Anjou, became increasingly beleaguered and was powerless to control either Catholic or Protestant factions.

In 1584, matters came to a head with the sudden death of the king's brother and heir,

Fourteenth-century fortifications guard the harbor of La Rochelle. A chain could be stretched between the towers to close the harbor at night. La Rochelle, a port on the Atlantic coast, was an important site of continued Huguenot resistance after the St. Bartholomew's Day Massacre.

HENRICVS VALOSE III D. G. FRANCIÆ ET POLONIÆ REX

QVI DEDIT ANTE DVAS TERTIAM ILLE DABIT CORONAM

Francis, duke of Anjou. Henry was childless, and the next in line to the throne was Henry of Navarre, who had reconverted to Protestantism. Threatened with the prospect of a Protestant king, the Catholics, led by another Henry, the duke of Guise, responded by forming the Sainte-Union, the Holy Union, or Catholic League.

The league made a secret treaty with Spain by which it agreed to take up arms against the Protestants in return for regular payments of Spanish cash. In March 1585, Guise issued the Declaration of Péronne, which protested against the Protestant tendencies of the Crown and called all true Catholics to arms against Protestantism. The much-weakened king had no choice but to accede to the league's demands. In July, he reluctantly signed the Treaty of Nemours, revoking all privileges previously granted to the Protestants.

Henry of Navarre rose to the Huguenots' defense, and a new, three-way civil war broke out, the so-called War of the Three Henries (1585–1589). In May 1588, a League uprising in Paris drove Henry III ignominiously from the capital. In December, the king struck back by having both the duke and the cardinal of Guise killed.

In February 1589, the king and Henry of Navarre temporarily joined forces to lay siege to the capital, which was still in the hands of the League. The people of Paris

rose up in fury against the king. Numerous Catholic pamphlets appeared, arguing—much as the Protestants had done earlier—that the king had forfeited his right to the throne. In this hysterical atmosphere, a fanatical young friar called Jacques Clément managed to gain access to the king at Saint-Cloud, just outside Paris, and stabbed him to death. The last Valois king died on August 1, 1589. One of his last acts was to recognize the Bourbon Henry of Navarre as his rightful successor.

The kingdom, however, was fragmenting. The league refused to recognize the new king, and in many regions—Brittany and Burgundy, for example—league aristocrats ruled independently of the crown. The people of Paris, moreover, refused to submit to Henry, who therefore continued his siege of the capital.

The Spanish Intervention

The succession of a Protestant king in France threatened a European war. Spain, in particular, feared that if France were lost to Protestantism, it would lose control of the Netherlands. Consequently, just as Henry IV seemed set to take Paris, Spanish troops, under Cardinal Farnese, invaded Brittany and, later, Languedoc.

In the following years, repeated Spanish interventions successfully frustrated the king's attempts to assert control. On the

An eighteenth-century colored engraving depicts the assassination of Henry III in comic-book style. The Dominican friar Jacques Clément, inflamed by anti-Valois propaganda, stabs the king in the stomach. The dying king leaves the throne to the kneeling Henry, king of Navarre, on condition that he convert to Catholicism. Clément, meanwhile, receives the death penalty. Henry III was the first French king to be assassinated—an indication of how far the mystique of the monarch had fallen since the beginning of the Wars of Religion.

A contemporary Spanish painting depicts the siege of Paris in 1590 by the forces of the new king, Henry IV. The capital resisted the Bourbon king for almost five years—it has been estimated that some 13,000 inhabitants died in the siege. The siege finally ended peacefully after the king reconverted to Catholicism at the abbey of Saint-Denis, just north of the city, in July 1593. Henry IV is reputed to have said: "Paris is well worth a mass."

other hand, Henry was able to exploit the traditional French mistrust of the Spanish to pose as the patriotic defender of French independence. Moderate Catholics—known disparagingly as *politiques* because they wanted to end the war for pragmatic, political reasons rather than religious principles—increasingly called for the country to unite under a strong monarch.

In July 1593, Henry finally removed the last rational grounds for refusing to recognize his kingship by reconverting to Catholicism at the abbey of Saint-Denis, north of Paris. He summed up his decision by saying, "Paris is well worth a mass." In March 1594, Henry was finally able to enter Paris without a shot being fired. Throughout the kingdom, the people rallied patriotically to his cause. By 1596, Henry IV had conquered, or at least appeased, the remaining league towns.

Henry IV and the Edict of Nantes

The Huguenots, for their part, were none too impressed by Henry's latest conversion, and their displeasure constantly threatened to tip France back into civil war. For a time, however, the continuing war with Spain prevented the king from addressing this difficult issue. It was only in April 1598, when he was engaged in peace negotiations with the Spanish, that Henry was able to issue the Edict of

Nantes, with which the Wars of Religion finally came to an end.

Under the edict, Henry granted every seigneur, or lord, the right to hold Protestant services within his own household. It allowed Protestant worship in one town in each county and in every town in which there was a Protestant majority. It banned Protestant worship, however, from cathedral cities and from the region around Paris. The edict also promised Protestants the same civil rights as Catholics. Finally, Protestants were granted control of a hundred fortified towns.

While the edict largely succeeded in pacifying Protestants, many Catholics did not accept it. Occasionally, Henry had to use force to implement it. Only as Catholic fears that the edict would create a Protestant "state within a state" abated did the edict become, almost by default, part of the status quo. A war in which religious and political motives were inextricable ended with an edict that was not so much an outbreak of cross-confessional cooperation as a weary recognition that France could not survive another decade of war.

Henry's was no mean achievement, however. The edict led France into a new period of prosperity, the cultural flowering of which would make the seventeenth century the Grand Siècle, or Great Century, of the French nation (*see 4:449*).

Tudor England

A Lasting Dynasty

In 1485, Henry Tudor (1457–1509) defeated and killed England's king Richard III at the Battle of Bosworth. Then twenty-eight years old, the victor claimed the throne and became Henry VII. He and his successors ruled England for more than a century. The age of the Tudors would later become popularly identified as one of the most glorious periods of English history.

The Wars of the Roses (1455–1485)

The Tudors' beginnings were not promising. For some thirty years, England had been periodically rocked by conflict for power between aristocratic factions. These so-called Wars of the Roses took their name from the crests of the two families at the heart of the conflict: the house of Lancaster was identified by a red rose, the house of York by a white rose.

The death of the Yorkist Richard III on the battlefield at Bosworth marked the end of the wars. Although Henry was related to the house of Lancaster, he set out to end the factional struggle. The new king was reconciliatory toward his defeated opponents. The crest he adopted included both white and red roses as a symbol of the harmony he wished to bring to the country.

An Underdeveloped Kingdom

Henry VII faced an enormous task. The wars had devastated agriculture and trade. Both sides had executed their opponents, effectively wiping out a generation of England's nobility. The monarchy lay in disrepute thanks to its involvement in factional struggles. Richard's predecessor, Edward IV, had tried to restore the power of the crown and bring stability to the country. England, however, remained underpopulated and underdeveloped compared with a power such as France. In commerce and culture, England lagged behind regions such as the Italian states or Flanders.

A detail from a painting by Nicholas Hilliard shows how the Tudor rose combined the white and red roses, symbols of the houses of York and Lancaster.

With so many of the nobility who traditionally made up parliament killed in the wars, Henry governed through a system of privy councils, or committees of advisers. The country was effectively run by the king and a small group of trusted ministers. This "household government" was a first step toward a modern administrative system.

Henry could not afford to offend the new nobility, made up of the wealthy merchants and farmers of the gentry class, who now wielded local power. With no standing army or police force, he relied on them to enforce laws or wage wars on his behalf. Henry consulted the gentry or magnates on questions of government in the King's Council, but the council's powers were limited. Financial matters, for example, remained in the hands of the inner circle.

Henry's resources were relatively meager, and he had to manage them well. The king was dedicated to his task, checking and signing every page of the treasury ledgers. Henry's financial management seemed mean and harsh to some people, but one historian called him "the best businessman ever to sit on the English throne."

Exercising Power

While Henry tried to appease the magnates by including them in the government, he was also quick to attack them if he felt that their local power was becoming too strong. So-called powers of attainder and forfeiture allowed the king to punish treason by confiscating magnates' castles and possessions. Because the power to make accusations of treason lay with the king and his councillors rather than the courts, Henry was effectively empowered to replace his opponents with his supporters.

As Henry VII centralized power, he also encouraged commerce. Partly to improve trade links, he married his daughter and his heir respectively into the Scottish and Spanish royal families. The Scottish were closely allied to the French, while the Spanish connection gave English wool traders easier access to the rich markets of the Spanish Netherlands.

The woolen industry flourished. Many landowners enclosed, or fenced in, their fields to graze sheep. The process drove landless farmers, or villeins, from the land they traditionally worked to join a growing

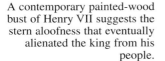

A contemporary painted-wood bust of Henry VII suggests the stern aloofness that eventually alienated the king from his people.

underclass in England's towns. The countryside became dominated by farmers of the gentry class.

A Change of Monarch

By the time Henry VII died in 1509, England's government was stable, and the country was growing more prosperous. The king's financial strictness had made him unpopular, however. His death was greeted with feasting, dancing, and celebration throughout the kingdom.

The new king, the eighteen-year-old Henry VIII (1491–1547), wanted to increase the power of the English crown. He had become heir on the death of his elder brother, Arthur, in 1502. Henry also married Arthur's widow, Catherine of Aragon, daughter of King Ferdinand of Spain.

Like his father, Henry VIII ruled with the help of a series of able ministers. The first, Thomas Wolsey, archbishop of York, was a butcher's son who had risen to become the most senior churchman in England. He was Henry's chief confidant and eventually became his lord chancellor. Wolsey reorganized the government, increasing the crown's ability to collects taxes, enforce laws, and maintain civil order. He also engineered a peace treaty between England and France, against whom Henry had fought a series of unsuccessful campaigns.

Challenge to the Pope

In 1527, Henry VIII launched a course of events with profound implications for British history. He asked the pope, Clement VII, to grant him a divorce from Catherine. Henry wanted a male heir, but Catherine, at forty-two, was too old to have more children and of her five babies only Mary Tudor had survived infancy. Henry wanted to marry his mistress, Anne Boleyn.

The annulment of royal marriages was not unknown, but the pope, backed by the Spanish king, refused to grant a divorce from the Spanish princess. Henry then insisted that the divorce be granted by English authorities, which brought him into conflict with Rome. Henry had only been able to marry his brother's widow with permission from an earlier pope. To insist now that the pope had no say in his divorce, Henry would have to show that the previous pope had no authority to allow him to marry in the first place. This would chal-

An aerial photograph of Hampton Court, on the outskirts of London. Thomas Wolsey built the palace, which passed to Henry VIII when Wolsey fell from office. The king enlarged the palace, which became his favorite residence.

Henry VIII painted by his court artist, Hans Holbein the Younger. Holbein helped design Henry's clothes and accessories, which were all intended to help promote his kingly image of wealth and power.

lenge the fundamental authority of the Catholic Church.

Cardinal Wolsey refused to grant the divorce without the pope's permission. His failure to negotiate a compromise between the two sides marked the end of Wolsey's power. Henry replaced him with Sir Thomas More, who resigned in 1532, and then with Thomas Cromwell.

Between 1532 and 1540, Cromwell instituted a series of laws that effectively destroyed the authority of the Catholic Church in England. The Act of Supremacy established a new church, the Church of England, with Henry at its head. When Thomas More himself refused to recognize

Henry's authority, the king had him executed. Henry confiscated vast amounts of church property. He "dissolved" England's monasteries and seized their land, along with valuable church artifacts. Henry sold most of this land and booty to the gentry, and used the proceeds to finance unsuccessful military expeditions in France.

These developments—called the "Henrician Reformation"—coincided with the rise of Protestantism in Europe (*see 2:151*). Although Henry's motives were political and he himself still believed in Catholic doctrine, the Anglican Church was not immune to the new Protestant ideas. Many of Henry's advisers were sympathetic to the

Protestant cause. More and more "reforming" or "dissenting" churches appeared in England, particularly in the ports that had greatest contact with the continent.

The Six Wives of Henry VIII

Henry's turbulent personal life continued. He married Anne Boleyn in 1533 but she did not give him the male heir he wanted so badly, only a daughter, Elizabeth. Before the Henrician reforms were even complete, Henry had divorced Anne, charged her with adultery, and had her executed. The king went on through a well-known succession of wives, six in all. After Anne came Jane Seymour, who bore the king's son, Edward. Seymour died following childbirth. Henry then married the Flemish princess Anne of Cleves to win European allies, but he did not find her attractive and soon divorced her. Catherine Howard, Henry's fifth wife, meddled in politics and was executed in 1542. Henry's final wife, Catherine Parr, survived his death in 1547.

Henry's Legacy

Henry VIII was the most powerful English king for centuries. Thanks to his ministers and his dominant personality, his control of England's political and religious institutions was virtually absolute. The civil order he maintained encouraged commerce and agriculture. The rural gentry bought church lands, and a new landed aristocracy began to emerge. Only in foreign policy did Henry prove unsuccessful. He spent most of the wealth he acquired from selling church property on fruitless foreign wars.

Elizabeth I (1533–1603)

After Henry's death the throne passed through the hands of three monarchs in a decade: Edward VI, Lady Jane Grey, and Mary Tudor (see 2:210). Mary reversed many of Henry's reforms in an attempt to return England to the Catholic faith. The accession in 1558 of Mary's half-sister Elizabeth did not seem to promise stability. The new queen faced religious division and a difficult international situation. With a gift for keeping people guessing about her intentions and an iron will, however, the young ruler triumphed over her difficulties.

Elizabeth's reign is often seen as a golden age in English history. The economy thrived, as did culture. The Elizabethan Age was the age of the playwrights William Shakespeare and Ben Jonson, the poet Edmund Spenser, and the adventurers Walter Raleigh and Francis Drake.

At the heart of England's prosperity lay steady population growth. There was ample

This crest marks the grave of Anne Boleyn in the Chapel Royal at the Tower of London. Anne, who was beheaded in 1536, remained a popular and tragic heroine in English history.

The ruins of Fountains Abbey in Yorkshire, one of many rich religious foundations destroyed in Henry's dissolution of the monasteries.

The five-year-old prince Edward, later Edward VI, holds a small monkey in a portrait by Hans Holbein the Younger.

The time between the death of Henry VIII in 1547 and the accession of Elizabeth I in 1558 provided a reminder of the instability that still threatened the achievements of the Tudor dynasty. The period was marked by infighting, religious strife, and an ultimately tragic attempt to change the line of inheritance to the throne.

Edward Tudor (1537–1553) became King Edward VI in 1547, at the age of only nine. The boy required a group of trusted advisers to run his government. The king's "protector" was his uncle, the duke of Somerset, a Protestant who was eager to see the Anglican Church drop Catholic practices in favor of Protestant rituals.

In 1549, Somerset's ally Thomas Cranmer, archbishop of Canterbury, published the first Anglican prayer book. It was in English rather than the Latin of Catholic rituals and was Protestant in its doctrines. Many English people were opposed to Protestant ideas, however, particularly in rural areas far from the centers of government power. Anti-prayer-book riots broke out in 1549 in Cornwall, Devon, and Norfolk. Meanwhile, Somerset had involved England in wars with France and Scotland.

In 1550, the earl of Warwick ousted Somerset in a coup. Warwick had his predecessor executed and declared himself duke of Northumberland. A crisis loomed. The fifteen-year-old king, who had always been sickly, was dying. After his death, the line of succession would see the crown pass to Mary Tudor (1516–1558), the Catholic daughter of Henry VIII and Catherine of Aragon. Before Edward died, however, Northumberland engineered the accession of Lady Jane Grey, his own daughter-in-law. Jane was the great-granddaughter of Henry VII, making her third in line to the throne after Mary Tudor and Elizabeth. Beautiful and intelligent, the fifteen-year-old fainted when she first heard about Northumberland's plan.

When Edward VI died on July 6, 1553, Lady Jane Grey reluctantly became queen. She was never crowned, however. She ruled for only nine days, the origin of the phrase "nine days' wonder." By asserting her right to the throne and by disguising

labor for agriculture and commerce. Merchant companies sent fishing expeditions to Greenland and the Grand Banks of Newfoundland (*see 3:388*). Wars on the continent (*see 2:225*) created a demand for imported grain, which led to a better balance between sheep raising and arable farming in England. Commerce offered displaced peasants new employment.

A Royal Image
Elizabeth was a very popular ruler. "Good Queen Bess" also carefully created her own cult of personality. Refusing to marry, the so-called Virgin Queen came to represent purity, compassion, and healing. She presented herself as the loving mother of her

the extent of her Catholic beliefs, Mary gained the support of the English gentry. She marched to London and overthrew Northumberland. He and his fellow plotters were eventually executed, including the tragic Lady Jane.

The new monarch had lived in Spain and France for nearly twenty years and was a devout Catholic. Mary sought to restore her religion to England and to reimpose the pope's authority. Parliament changed the laws readily, insisting only that Mary would not reclaim the church lands sold to them by Henry VIII. Mary also reformed the system for collecting customs money, increasing the Crown's income.

Mary is most remembered, however, for persecuting Protestants. "Bloody Mary" had more than three hundred people burned at the stake, including Archbishop Cranmer. Mary's welcome from her subjects disappeared as her repression grew more brutal. A popular book, John Foxe's *Book of Martyrs*, made heroes of Cranmer and the other victims. Many Protestants fled into exile in Europe, where they bombarded England with anti-Catholic propaganda. Queen Mary also alienated the English when she married Philip, heir to the Habsburg Spanish throne, in 1554.

The marriage brought the threat that England would be controlled by the Catholic Habsburgs. A violent uprising against the marriage failed to have any effect. When Philip became king of Spain in 1556, England was soon dragged into Spanish affairs. Mary joined her husband in a war against France. England's disastrous involvement led to the loss of Calais, an English port in northern France that had been a valuable center of the wool trade.

Before the crisis worsened, however, Mary died in 1558. As she and Philip had no heir, the Habsburgs lost their claim to the English crown. On November 17, 1558, Elizabeth I ascended the throne. After ten years of upheaval, the Tudors once again brought stability to England.

Mary Tudor holds a Tudor rose in a portrait by a Spanish artist from 1554.

211

kingdom. The queen was also a strong ruler, however, declaring: "I know I have the body of a weak and feeble woman, but I have the heart and stomach of a king, and of a king of England too."

Foremost among Elizabeth's problems was growing tension between Catholics and Protestants. Protestant ideas had become increasingly popular, due in part to increased trade with European centers of religious reform, such as Amsterdam. The queen steered the Anglican Church toward a moderately Protestant theology and instructed that services be conducted in English rather than the traditional Latin. She also retained some Catholic ceremonies and refused to persecute people for their private beliefs. The queen's compromise did not satisfy everyone, however. Catholics resented the power of the Anglican Church, while militant Protestants objected to anything that suggested the toleration of Catholicism.

A portrait by Nicholas Hilliard of Elizabeth I shows how the queen reinforced her royal image with elaborate dresses and jewels. Elizabeth tried to control all portraits of herself and turned her public appearances into displays of wealth and power.

A contemporary painting shows the Battle of Gravelines, the confused naval encounter in which the English Royal Navy defeated Spain's Armada.

Rumors of Catholic plots to seize the throne grew louder after the assassination in 1584 of William of Orange, Europe's other great Protestant leader. The English executed Catholics suspected of plotting against the crown.

Tudor Ireland

England's religious tension echoed other tensions in Europe. Elizabeth sent troops to help the Protestant Dutch in their rebellion against their Catholic Spanish rulers (*see 2:215*). England also came into conflict with Spain in Ireland. After three centuries of trying to conquer the island, the English only controlled the Pale, the area around Dublin. Henry VIII declared himself king of Ireland in 1541 and made his new domain subject to English law. Irish Catholics fled to the continent, while English and Scottish settlers took their place. But the Tudors still did not fully control the island. The Irish chiefs held the balance of power.

The Spanish, meanwhile, encouraged the Irish to a series of rebellions. In 1588, the hostility between England and Spain came to a head. Provoked by the execution of Mary, Queen of Scots, and by English raids on Spanish ports, King Philip II sent his Armada, or navy, to carry troops from the Netherlands to invade England (*see 2:194*).

The Armada

The Armada was said to be invincible. When they met the Royal Navy, however, the Spanish ships could not force the English into battle on their own terms. Trapped in a narrow part of the English Channel and harried by enemy vessels, the Armada fled. A storm wrecked many of the Spanish vessels and dispersed the rest.

England had only narrowly survived. Although Elizabeth was ill prepared militarily and financially to fight Spain, the defeat of the Armada confirmed England's emergence as a great power. It also sig-

Little Moreton Hall in Cheshire, England, is an original example of the typical black-and-white timbered houses built by the new wealthy gentry during the Tudor period.

naled the end of Spanish influence in Ireland. In 1603, England's conquest of Ireland was completed when the last great Irish rebel, Hugh O'Neill, surrendered.

Tudor Scotland

Scotland, England's northern neighbor, was traditionally allied to Catholic France. The Tudor monarchs therefore faced the potential threat of having to fight simultaneous wars in the north and south. In 1502, to negate this possibility, Henry VII had signed a perpetual peace with the Scots. The Scots broke the treaty in 1513, during one of Henry VIII's wars with France, but were utterly defeated at the Battle of Flodden. Some thirty years later, Henry responded to the close alliance of King James V with the French by again crushing the Scots, this time at Solway Moss. James died soon after.

Scotland's new ruler, the Catholic queen Mary, married the heir to the French throne. Under the influence of the preacher John Knox, however, many of the Scottish nobility had adopted Presbyterianism, a radical form of Protestantism. In 1567, these anti-Catholic, anti-French nobles forced Mary to abdicate. She fled south to England, but she found only temporary sanctuary with her cousin, Elizabeth I. English Protestants suspected that Catholics plotted to make Mary queen instead of Elizabeth. After a long imprisonment, Mary was beheaded in 1587.

The new Scottish king, Mary's son James VI (1566–1625), joined Knox and the nobles to rid Scotland of French influence. James's cousin, Elizabeth I, gave the Scots some help by campaigning against the French.

When Elizabeth died childless in 1603, James VI inherited her throne as James I of England, peacefully uniting England and Scotland under his Stuart dynasty. This peaceful succession was perhaps Elizabeth's greatest achievement, given the turbulent recent past of the English crown. But beneath the glories of Elizabethan England, problems were building up that would have grave consequences for the Stuart kings (*see 2:235*).

James VI of Scotland in a portrait painted in 1605, soon after he had ascended to the English throne as James I.

The Revolt of
the Netherlands

The Eighty Years' War

When the Habsburg king Philip II inherited the throne of Spain from his father, Emperor Charles V, in 1556, he inherited the greatest empire in Europe (*see 2:183*). The richest of Philip's lands were the Low Countries, present-day Holland and Belgium. Far from the center of imperial power in Spain, the Spanish Netherlands thrived. They were one of the two most urbanized parts of the continent; their towns and cities controlled half of Europe's trade. Their income was vital for maintaining Philip's empire. Within a decade of his accession, however, the Spanish king faced open revolt in the Netherlands. Philip's Dutch subjects fought for their independence in a war that lasted eighty years.

Habsburg Centralization

Philip's Habsburg family acquired the provinces of the Low Countries at the end of the fifteenth century, when they were part of Burgundy. Dutch taxes helped fund the military struggle to build their Spanish-Austrian empire in the first half of the sixteenth century. To raise tax revenue and increase their authority, the Habsburgs appointed successive governors-general to the provinces. They established a capital at Brussels in Flanders in the southern Netherlands and sought support from the nobles who ruled the Dutch provinces.

The people of the Low Countries did not welcome centralized government. The region included a patchwork of seventeen

A sixteenth-century painting of Antwerp shows the town's fishmarket and harbor. Trade and shipping made the Low Countries one of Europe's richest regions.

Hunters return to a snow-covered village in a 1565 painting by Pieter Brueghel the Elder. Harsh winters caused food shortages and inflation, increasing Dutch resentment of the Spanish.

small provinces, each with its own traditions. People saw themselves as citizens of their own province rather than of the Netherlands. The northern, Dutch-speaking provinces tended to rely on agriculture and fishing, while the southern, mainly French-speaking provinces were more urbanized. Antwerp, in the south, was one of Europe's greatest trade centers.

The only centralized power in the region lay in an assembly, the States General, in which each province was represented by its leading nobles. The States General was a powerful body that controlled the raising of revenue. Its members were afraid of losing their traditional privileges but unwilling to pay taxes to fund Habsburg wars. Throughout the century, the States General opposed Habsburg efforts at centralization. Troops had to be sent from Spain to quash resistance to high taxation.

Economic Crisis

After Philip II came to the throne in 1556, tension heightened between ruler and ruled. The Low Countries were in a state of economic and religious crisis. The sixteenth century was a time of great inflation in Europe, and in the Low Countries the inflation was made worse by a series of harsh winters, poor harvests, and devastating floods that caused food shortages. A Spanish war against France drained the economy until the war ended in 1559. By then, thousands of artisans in the towns were on the brink of starvation. The urban elites resented the Spanish governor's alliance with a handful of wealthy rural noblemen at the expense of the towns.

Although they were often Catholics, the nobles were also distrustful of the Spanish. Their own wealth was closely connected with that of the traders and merchants in the towns. Those town dwellers were often Protestants, however. The reformed faith gained a strong foothold among the business class of the Low Countries in the first half of the century. Groups such as the Anabaptists and Calvinists opposed the practices of the Catholic Church and the rule of Spain. Philip II, meanwhile, was committed to protecting the Catholic faith. He planned to use the brutal tactics of the Spanish Inquisition to eliminate Protes-

In *The Usurers*, painted around 1509, the Dutch artist Marinus Van Reymersae depicts a pair of moneylenders in their office. The artist intended the painting to reveal the sin of greed and materialism.

tantism in the north (*see 2:173*). The Catholic nobles of the Netherlands, however, were reluctant to see the persecution of Protestants on whom much of the health of the Dutch economy depended.

The Council of Blood

Dutch resentment of Spanish rule led to a call for religious toleration. When Philip II refused the request, the tension in the Low Countries erupted into violence. During the summer of 1566, Calvinist crowds stormed Catholic churches, destroying sacred images. In response, Philip II appointed a new governor-general to the Netherlands, the duke of Alva (1508–1582). Alva, a skilled and experienced general, arrived in Brussels in 1568 with orders to impose severe penalties upon religious dissenters.

Alva launched a ruthless campaign of repression, beheading and burning Protestants at the stake and confiscating their property. The body that passed the sentences, the Council of Troubles, became known as the Council of Blood. Alva spared no one. His victims included two powerful noblemen who had called for reli-

An anonymous contemporary portrait of Ferdinand, duke of Alva, shows the nobleman in his armor. Appointed governor-general of the Netherlands in 1568, Alva led the campaign against Dutch Protestants.

William of Orange, painted in 1555. The nobleman was known as William the Silent for his ability to restrain any outbursts of temper.

pose a new property tax. This tax would have stripped the States General of its power to control revenue and would have been the final step in centralizing Spanish rule.

William of Orange
Among those leaving the Low Countries was William I, prince of Orange (1533–1584), who retired to land he owned in Germany. As the stadtholder, or governor, of the province of Holland, William had argued against imposing religious unity on the Low Countries. One of Europe's richest men, William had been born to Protestant parents but raised a Roman Catholic at the governor's court in Brussels. He was horrified by Alva's religious persecution and wanted to unite Protestants and Catholics in opposition to Spanish authority.

With the help of his influential relatives, William raised an army among the Protestant states of Germany. He invaded the Netherlands in 1568, and although he was defeated, this decisive action made him the popular symbol of Dutch resistance to Spanish rule.

Foreign Affairs
Back in Germany, where he formally joined the Lutheran Church, William planned another offensive. Meanwhile events in the Low Countries were being watched closely by other states. William had an alliance with France, where sympathizers raised a Protestant force to support his invasion. In Protestant England, meanwhile, some courtiers believed that the English should back the Dutch in order to weaken Spanish power (*see 2:205*). Rebellious Dutch seamen, called the Sea

Cannons, such as this bronze example cast in Flanders around the end of the Eighty Years' War, were a vital weapon in a campaign largely based on siege warfare.

gious reform. The counts of Egmond and Hoorne were beheaded in Brussels in 1568. Alva put their severed heads in a box and sent them to Philip in Madrid.

To escape Alva, many Dutch Protestants fled to the north; others escaped to England. Nearly two percent of all citizens left the country. Alva also attempted to im-

Beggars, used English harbors as bases from which to disrupt Alva's supply ships in the English Channel.

William planned to launch his offensive in the summer of 1572, but events forced him into action sooner than he wanted. The English expelled the Sea Beggars, who had become difficult to control and were even attacking English ships in the North Sea. On April 1, 1572, the Dutch privateers captured the port of Brielle in southern Holland. The following week, another raid from the sea captured the strategic port of Flushing. The Sea Beggars advanced inland and sparked off popular uprisings in favor of William. Town after town selected William as stadtholder.

Vicious War

While the Sea Beggars moved inland, the duke of Alva withdrew his troops. As William speeded up his invasion plans, Alva moved his forces south to face him and his French allies. After much indecision, King Charles IX of France had given permission for 15,000 Frenchmen to invade the Netherlands. On the night of August 23, 1572, however, some 3,000 French Protestants died in Paris in the Massacre of St. Bartholomew (*see 2:201*). Among them was Admiral Coligny, leader of the force. The French Huguenots could not now help the Dutch.

William of Orange joined forces with the Sea Beggars as they raised revolts in the towns throughout the central provinces of Holland and Zeeland. For the next four years the provinces became a battlefield as Spanish forces counterattacked from the south. Alva himself, however, was recalled to Spain on his own request in 1573.

The Spanish besieged the Dutch in their walled cities and starved them into surrender. Haarlem fell after a seven-month siege. The town of Leiden survived only because William ordered the dikes to be opened to flood the camps of the besieging Spanish troops. In 1576, in the "Fury of Antwerp," Spanish troops killed 7,000 citizens of the city in eleven days.

In that same year, stubborn Dutch resistance drove the Spanish governor to the bargaining table. The result was the short-lived Pacification of Ghent, which seemed to restore the rights of Dutch Protestants and provide home rule. The next governor, Don John of Austria, soon reneged on the agreement and hostilities resumed.

A sixteenth-century engraving depicts the aftermath of the long siege of Haarlem, which surrendered in July 1573.

The Two Unions

William's resistance relied on the collaboration of both Catholics and Calvinists. That collaboration ended in 1578. The Union of Arras reconciled the southern provinces of Flanders, present-day Belgium, with Spain. Those predominantly Catholic provinces feared the growing influence of intolerant Calvinist Protestantism to their north.

The following year, the Union of Utrecht brought together the six leading states of the northern provinces to form a "closer union" within the States General. In effect, the agreement marked the foundation of a new and separate nation.

A book illustration from the nineteenth century shows the assassination of William of Orange by the Frenchman Balthazar Gérard in 1584.

Orange was assassinated by a fanatical French Catholic. Philip II had encouraged this murder in the hope of ending the Dutch rebellion. Despite William's death and a series of military defeats in Flanders, the United Provinces continued their struggle. The States General, which had formerly met in the Flemish city of Brussels, now began to assemble in the Hague in the United Provinces.

The Duke of Parma

The arrival of a new Spanish governor signaled another blow to the Dutch cause. Alessandro Farnese (1545–1592), the Italian duke of Parma, was a shrewd commander of great bravery. During the siege of Oudenaarde in 1582, it was said, he gave orders for a table to be set up so that he and his staff could dine outside. A cannonball from inside the town blew off the head of one of the diners; a fragment of his skull pierced another officer's eye. A second ball killed two more officers. Parma arranged the removal of the dead, ordered the table relaid, and continued the meal.

Ill-Fated Intervention

With Parma's armies in control of Flanders and progressing north, the States General sought assistance from foreign powers. They approached first Henry III of France and then Elizabeth I of England. The queen offered some protection in the form of Robert Dudley (c. 1532–1588), earl of Leicester, who arrived in the Netherlands in 1585 with a small force. His arrival gave a great boost to Dutch morale. The following year, the States General named him governor-general. The English nobleman determined to establish himself as absolute ruler of the country. He had the support of many Calvinist leaders and was popular in the smaller provinces, which feared domination by the largest, Holland. Dudley's attempt to invade Holland in 1587 was a fiasco, however, and he abandoned his efforts. The States General put aside hopes of foreign protection and determined to become an independent state.

Maurice of Nassau

The office of chief stadtholder now fell to William of Orange's younger son, Prince Maurice of Nassau (1567–1625). With the assistance of his adviser, Johan van Oldenbarnevelt (1547–1619), the eighteen-year-old ruler set about reorganizing the Dutch army. Like other armies of the time, it was a largely mercenary force of many nationalities. To combat the ever-present threat of mutiny, Maurice increased his soldiers'

Known briefly as the Dutch Republic and later as the United Provinces of the Netherlands, the new nation remained in many ways a confederation of independent states. The provinces agreed to cooperate to resist Spanish domination, but each remained sovereign in domestic affairs. All decisions on war and taxation had to be unanimous. The agreement did not renounce the sovereignty of the Spanish king but did confirm the authority of local governors to rule the provinces.

The agreement paved the way for the dominance of the Calvinist Dutch Reformed Church in the northern provinces. Catholic northerners migrated south, while Calvinist southerners fled north. The Low Countries split between the predominantly Calvinist United Provinces to the north and the mainly Roman Catholic Flanders.

The campaign for independence received a second blow in 1584, when William of

pay. He equipped his soldiers with identical muskets and drilled them in rapid and disciplined use of their weapons. He instructed his officers in siege warfare and methodically beset the Spanish strongholds one at a time.

The Spanish, meanwhile, angered by Dudley's expedition and the execution of the Catholic Mary, Queen of Scots, planned an attack on England. In 1588, the great fleet, the Armada, sailed north from Spain. The plan was to ship Parma's troops across the English Channel. Parma stopped fighting the Dutch and gathered his men on the coast, but the troops left before the Armada arrived. When the Armada did arrive it was met in the Channel by the English navy and then scattered by bad weather. The planned invasion came to nothing.

In 1590, Philip sent Parma to attack northern France. Maurice, meanwhile, won back a number of cities in the northern provinces. Two years later, Parma died from wounds received fighting the French. Maurice attempted to fan a rebellion in Flanders in an effort to reunite the northern

and southern provinces. The largely Catholic southerners did not support him, and Maurice gave up in 1607. The new nation agreed to a truce in 1609 in which

Prince Maurice's troops meet the Spanish in the Battle of Nijmegen in 1585 in this contemporary oil painting. Maurice's reforms to military training and organization made the Dutch a formidable fighting force.

This delftware vase has spouts for individual tulips. In the early seventeenth century, Holland experienced a "tulip mania," during which the price of bulbs rocketed: one single bulb was exchanged for a flourishing brewery. Prices crashed dramatically in 1637, bringing financial ruin to many Dutch families.

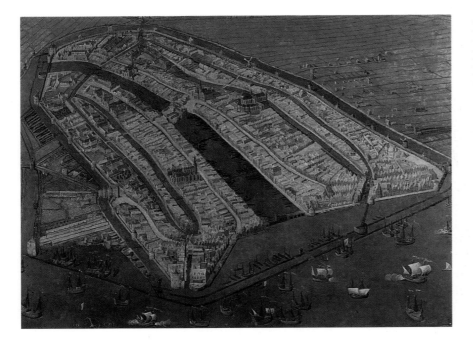

A view of Amsterdam painted in 1538 shows the city before its great expansion. Less than a hundred years later, the city's population had risen to 105,000 and a series of canals had been built to drain low-lying land to allow the city to expand.

View of Delft by Jan Vermeer (mid-seventeenth century). Although Vermeer was best known for interior views, his few townscapes celebrated the Netherlands' urban life, based on trade, canals, and shipping.

Spain recognized the independence of the Republic. The truce lasted until 1621, when the Dutch, like most of Europe, were swept up in the Thirty Years' War (*see 2:225*).

The New Economy

The new nation's military victories would have been impossible without the rise of Dutch sea trade in the late sixteenth and early seventeenth centuries. Located on important trade routes, the United Provinces emerged as the dominant shipping nation in Europe. Amsterdam, the Dutch capital, replaced Antwerp as the continent's leading port. Antwerp had long been in decline; economic upheaval had interrupted its main sources of income, the Portuguese spice trade and the English cloth trade. During the Dutch Revolt, the United Provinces blockaded the Scheldt River leading to the port. The blockade was the final blow to Antwerp's prosperity. The city's population halved between 1550 and 1590, as many of its citizens moved north to settle in Amsterdam.

Dutch ships transported grain and military equipment from the Baltic Sea to the Mediterranean and returned with wines and manufactured goods. The German states shipped exports down the Rhine to Amsterdam. The majority of French exports were carried in Dutch ships. Even Spain depended on the Netherlands for grain and naval stores. In the early seventeenth century, the Dutch opened up the spice trade with the East Indies (*see 3:323*). While a large part of the Dutch economy remained tied to North Sea fishing, the new trade brought vast sums of money flooding into the Netherlands.

New institutions were needed to handle this increased trade. A modern banking system emerged. The Amsterdam exchange bank, founded in 1609, became a deposit

A 1631 oil painting by Cornelis de Vos shows a Dutch merchant's family. The subjects' stiff, sober clothes were typical of those adopted by well-to-do families of the rising middle classes.

bank for those engaged in sea trade. Large-scale industry appeared, as shipbuilders and sugar refiners tried to meet the demand for commercial exports. The population had grown rapidly in the sixteenth century, and land and food remained in high demand. Ambitious reclamation projects drained and diked coastal lands and transformed them into farmland and pasture.

Society and Culture

The Dutch sea trade of the seventeenth century supported one of the wealthiest nations in Europe. Much of society enjoyed a high standard of living. Merchants and financiers in the towns amassed great fortunes. They invested in real estate and government bonds, drove up the price of land, spurred on the construction of state-sponsored projects such as dikes, and assured the financial stability of the military. Artisans, tradesmen, and people in the nautical trades, such as shipbuilders and fishermen, also prospered by producing goods and services for this new elite. Dutch farmers thrived as the increasingly urban population demanded food and raw materials. In contrast, the traditionally important landed nobility gained only marginally from the new wealth. Their relative influence in the nation declined.

Domestic Pride

One of the distinguishing features of the so-called Golden Age of Dutch history was an increased sense of national pride. Both

the doctrines of Calvinism and the success of the rising middle classes taught ordinary Dutch people to value hard work, thrift, and honesty. The larger Dutch towns also developed an increasingly international character as a result of the sea trade and their toleration of religious minorities. Among those who settled in the Netherlands, for example, were dissenters from England, who would later found the New World colony of Plymouth, and Sephardic Jews, who fled persecution in Spain and Portugal. These outsiders were permitted economic and religious freedom but were denied political rights.

Cultural Center

The Golden Age also saw Dutch contributions to the arts, literature, and science that made the Netherlands a cultural focus of Europe. Economic prosperity financed this flowering, and the new nation's sense of purpose and ambition sustained its cultural community. Many poems and engravings, for example, recorded episodes of bravery, hardship, and sacrifice from the war against Spain.

This phenomenon was most visible in painting. The merchant class adorned their homes with Dutch landscapes and images of popular life that celebrated the values of hard work and sober, modest living. Amsterdam, Delft, and Haarlem emerged as cultural centers.

The period is best remembered for the work of the two greatest Dutch masters,

The Night Watch by
Rembrandt van Rijn, 1642.
Rembrandt's famous oil
painting showed the
businessmen who
commissioned the picture as
though they were a militia
patrol during the revolt over
half a century earlier.

Rembrandt van Rijn (1606–1669) of Amsterdam and Jan Vermeer (1632–1675) from Delft. Both these artists depicted uniquely Dutch scenes and often selected wealthy urban merchants for their models. Rembrandt's *The Night Watch,* for example, glorifies this new business class by portraying its members as a militia unit on patrol during the Dutch Revolt. Vermeer's paintings, meanwhile, were often intimate domestic scenes that celebrated the comfortable, orderly, and sober lives of the urban population.

Not many people got to enjoy such works, however. High culture was the province of the wealthy elite. Paintings were kept in private homes. Only a small part of the population was literate. Music, particularly organ music, was the only widely available form of culture. The strict Dutch Reformed Church, however, looked unfavorably on organ music, and eventually banned it from services. The one cultural figure who enjoyed widespread popularity was the poet and playwright Joost van den Vondel (1587–1679), whose biblical plays emphasized the importance of hard work and thrift.

Scientific Advances

While painting in the Golden Age overshadowed advances in other fields, the United Provinces made significant contributions to the so-called scientific revolution (*see 2:265*). The mathematician Simon Stevin (1548–1620) popularized the use of decimals in arithmetic. He also laid the groundwork for Isaac Newton's theory of gravity by disproving the belief that heavy bodies fall faster than lighter ones. Christiaan Huygens (1629–1695) helped explain how pendulums work, while Antonie van Leeuwenhoek (1632–1723) pioneered the use of the microscope.

A remarkable contribution to philosophy came from Baruch Spinoza (1632–1677). A lens grinder whose family was among the Jews who fled Portugal for Amsterdam, Spinoza pioneered a mathematical and rational view of the universe. His beliefs were so radical that his own Jewish community expelled him in 1656 for heresy. Such was the tolerant nature of the United Provinces, however, that he was able to live and work there freely until he died from tuberculosis, made worse by glass dust in his lungs.

The Thirty Years' War

From Religious Strife to "Reason of State"

The Thirty Years' War (1618–1648) was the culmination of the hundred or so years of religious strife between Catholics and Protestants that had occupied much of Europe since the Reformation. The war and its concluding peace changed European history for good. What began as a purely local affair—a dispute between the Catholic emperor of the Holy Roman Empire and his Protestant subjects in the kingdom of Bohemia—escalated into a Europe-wide war in which each country's political or strategic advantage rather than religious persuasion became the main motivating force.

A Divided Empire

In the seventeenth century, Germany was not a stable or unified state but a loose collection of more than a thousand semi-independent principalities, bishoprics, and free cities, united only by a shared nominal allegiance to the Holy Roman emperor.

Since the Reformation (*see 2:151*), these polities, or political units, had been divided between two hostile camps, Catholics and Lutheran Protestants. The Catholics predominated south of the Danube River, the Lutherans northeast of the Elbe River, while in between was a complex and explosive patchwork comprising both Catholics and Protestants. Since the Peace of Augsburg of 1555, an uneasy truce had existed between the two factions, but intense mutual suspicion remained.

The Holy Roman emperor was not a hereditary ruler. He was elected by seven of the most powerful German princes and archbishops, called the electors. Although in theory the electors might choose any prince as emperor, even a Protestant, in practice the powerful Catholic Habsburg family had a near monopoly on the title. The Habsburgs had many lands of their own in Germany and Austria, which they ruled from Vienna. Another branch of the family

This engraving shows the Battle of Lützen, 1632, at which imperial forces under Wallenstein defeated the army of the Swedish king Gustavus Adolphus. Contemporary engravings and woodcuts brought recent developments in the Thirty Years' War to the attention of a news-hungry European public.

A seventeenth-century engraving of the Defenestration of Prague, in which Protestants threw two Catholic members of Ferdinand I's regency council out of one of the windows of Prague Castle and thereby sparked the Thirty Years' War.

This engraving from 1699 depicts the aftermath of the Battle of the White Mountain of 1620, as imperial troops torture and punish Bohemian Protestants.

ruled Spain and was usually willing to assist the German branch with financial or military support in order to preserve both Habsburg and Catholic predominance in central Europe.

At the end of the sixteenth century, the Catholic rulers became more militant in imposing the legal principle of *cujus regio, ejus religio*, which gave a ruler the power to dictate the religion of his subjects. Many Protestants were forced either to convert to Catholicism or to go into exile. It was in part in response to this renewed Catholic effort that, in 1608, the elector Frederick IV of the Palatinate (1574–1610) and Christian, prince of Anhalt (1568–1630), formed a defensive alliance of Protestant

princes. This alliance, the Protestant Union, had the covert support of England and, perhaps more surprisingly, Catholic France. The French Bourbon monarchy was ready to take any opportunity to reduce Habsburg power in Germany. The Catholic duke of Bavaria, Maximilian (1573–1651), responded by forming the Catholic League, which inevitably drew the support of the papacy and Spain.

To complicate matters further, Spain's northern subjects, the Dutch, who were predominantly Protestant, were engaged in a long struggle for independence. This made them willing conspirators against the Habsburgs, eager to exploit any opportunity in Germany that might embroil the Spanish in a central European war.

The Crisis in Bohemia

Bohemia provided the spark that ignited this explosive situation. Bohemia, which later became part of Czechoslovakia, was part of the empire but was also a kingdom in its own right. While its king was Catholic, its population was largely Protestant. Under the Letter of Majesty established in 1609, Protestants' rights were protected by a parliament, the Estates.

In 1617, the Austrian Habsburgs decided that the staunchly Catholic Archduke Ferdinand of Inner Austria (1578–1637) should be groomed to succeed to the position of emperor and hoped first to have him placed as king of Bohemia. Because the Protestants there could not agree on an alternative candidate, the Bohemian estates reluctantly agreed to accept Ferdinand, but only on the condition that he continue to respect Protestant rights.

The Defenestration of Prague

It soon became clear that Ferdinand had no intention of honoring his promise. Soon after his succession late in 1617, he created an overwhelmingly Catholic council to rule on his behalf. The council began to carry out repressive measures against the Protestants, banning their books and forbidding Protestant worship on land owned by the Catholic Church.

On May 23, 1618, a delegation of some two hundred men from the Estates forcibly entered the regency council chamber, high up in a tower of Prague Castle. They accused the four Catholic members of the regency council who happened to be there of betraying the spirit of the Letter of Majesty. Tempers frayed, and the intruders ended up seizing two of the Catholic deputies and their secretary and throwing them headlong out of the tower window.

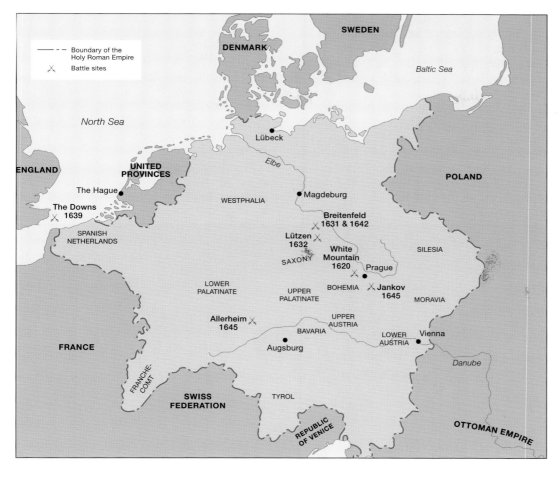

SWEDEN

DENMARK

Baltic Sea

North Sea

Lübeck

ENGLAND

UNITED PROVINCES

Elbe

POLAND

The Hague

WESTPHALIA

Magdeburg

The Downs
✕ 1639

Breitenfeld
✕ 1631 & 1642

SPANISH NETHERLANDS

Lützen
1632 ✕

White Mountain
1620

SILESIA

SAXONY

Prague

LOWER PALATINATE

UPPER PALATINATE

BOHEMIA

✕ Jankov
1645

MORAVIA

FRANCE

Allerheim
1645 ✕

UPPER AUSTRIA

BAVARIA

LOWER AUSTRIA

Vienna

FRANCHE-COMTÉ

Augsburg

Danube

SWISS FEDERATION

TYROL

REPUBLIC OF VENICE

OTTOMAN EMPIRE

This map shows the sites of the major battles of the Thirty Years' War.

All three men survived the sixty-foot drop. The incident served, however, as a dramatic declaration of independence by Bohemia's Protestants.

In the wake of the incident—known as the Defenestration of Prague—the Estates set up a provisional governing council, mobilized an army, and secured the support of other dissatisfied kingdoms of the empire, including Silesia, Moravia, and Upper and Lower Austria. By May 1619, the Bohemian rebels were laying siege to the Archduke Ferdinand in Vienna. They made another bold move by offering the Bohemian crown to Frederick V of the Palatinate. Although the prince's advisers warned him that acceptance would certainly unleash a general religious war, Frederick had himself crowned king of Bohemia in October 1619.

The Battle of the White Mountain

Frederick's advisers were proved right. Recognizing the danger the loss of Bohemia represented to Habsburg interests, the Spanish invaded the Palatinate—Frederick's primary German lands situated in the west of Germany—using forces that were already busy trying to control the Dutch revolt (*see 2:215*). The Spanish assault gave the emperor just the opportu-

nity he needed. In the Battle of the White Mountain, just outside Prague, on November 8, 1620, an imperial army defeated the Protestant forces under Christian of Anhalt. Frederick fled north and eventually found refuge at the Dutch court.

Emboldened by their victory, the imperial forces set about turning Bohemia into a Catholic kingdom. Protestants found their freedom of religion restricted or abolished, their rights suppressed, and their property seized. In the 1620s, over two-thirds of the property in Bohemia changed hands, and Protestants left the kingdom in the thousands. The Habsburgs had greatly strengthened their position.

Denmark Enters the Fray

The war was only temporarily in abeyance. The Dutch Republic was especially uneasy about the presence of Spanish troops over the border in Germany. A twelve-year truce that had given the Dutch a temporary respite from its long struggle with Spain was due to expire in April 1621, and they feared a combined Spanish and imperial onslaught on their territory. The Dutch prepared to defend themselves. In addition to harboring Frederick's court in exile, the Dutch also openly encouraged several of the Protestant German princes to resist the emperor and attempted to negotiate an international alliance against Spain.

In response to a concerted military offensive by Spain against them on land and sea, beginning in 1625, the Dutch organized the Coalition of the Hague, which included James I, king of England and Frederick's father-in-law, the princes of the North German states, and, most crucially, the Danish king, Christian IV (1577–1684), who offered to lead the new alliance. France, too, aided the coalition through its 1624 defensive treaty with the Dutch.

In reality, however, the English, French, and even the Dutch themselves actually gave little practical military support to the coalition. As a consequence, Christian, who himself had territorial ambitions on the northern reaches of the empire, was left to his own devices. For this reason, the period from 1626 until Christian's defeat in 1629 is sometimes called the Danish phase of the war.

Lined up against the coalition was the army of the Catholic League, under the military leadership of Jean t'Serclaes,

Gustavus Adolphus, king of Sweden, was a champion of the Protestant cause in the Thirty Years' War. Gustavus, a skilled military leader, helped Sweden reach its greatest power. The king died at the Battle of Lützen in 1632.

228

This later engraving shows an early-seventeenth-century German musketeer of the kind who fought during the Thirty Years' War. The soldier's musket was fired by touching a match to a hole in the breech to ignite the gunpowder charge.

baron Tilly (1559–1632). The emperor Ferdinand did not entirely trust Tilly, however, and so Ferdinand also turned for help to one of his richest subjects, the Czech Albrecht of Valstejn (1583–1634), or Wallenstein as he was known. Wallenstein had recently made himself spectacularly rich by dealing in property seized from the Protestants in Bohemia. His wealth meant that he was able to raise at his own expense an army of some 25,000 men to fight on the emperor's behalf.

Wallenstein's Influence

The combined imperial and league armies used their overwhelming numerical superiority to crush the forces of Christian and his German allies. Wallenstein, moreover, proved himself a master strategist. By April 1628, he had completed a spectacular advance to the shores of the Baltic Sea. By June that year, he had forced the beleaguered king of Denmark to sign the Treaty of Lübeck.

The outright Catholic victory encouraged Ferdinand to impose what he hoped would be a final religious settlement on the empire. In March 1629, he issued the Edict of Restitution, intending to use the armies of Tilly and Wallenstein to enforce its pro-Catholic dictates. These included the recovery of all property taken from the Catholic Church since the Treaty of Augsburg in 1555 and a complete ban on the practice of Calvinism.

The edict proved unwise. The stringency of its measures provoked widespread opposition. Resentment was only increased by the brutality with which Wallenstein's and Tilly's soldiers set about enforcing the edict. Like the troops of most contemporary European armies, which were largely composed of mercenaries, many of the soldiers were little better than bullies, thieves, and looters. The edict provided an easy target for Protestant propagandists.

Wallenstein's growing power rankled the empire's Catholic princes, too. They refused to recognize Ferdinand's son—later Ferdinand III (1608–1657)—as heir presumptive to the imperial crown unless the emperor dismissed Wallenstein and drastically cut the size of Wallenstein's huge and expensive army. In August 1630, the emperor complied, and Wallenstein retired to his estates in Bohemia.

The Swedish Phase of the War

Once again, the war was reignited by the ambitions of a Protestant king from outside the borders of the empire. In July 1630, a force led by the Swedish king Gustavus Adolphus (1594–1632) crossed the Baltic and landed in northern Germany, with the declared intention of "saving the liberties of empire" and preventing the loss of further Protestant lands. Gustavus Adolphus was an extremely competent military leader and in the preceding years had greatly increased Swedish military power and prestige. By a masterstroke of diplomacy, moreover, he had won the concrete backing of France—which hoped to contain an overpowerful Habsburg empire—for his German enterprise.

The Destruction of Magdeburg

The Protestant princes hesitated to give Gustavus their open support. They were suspicious of his objectives and were in any case by now far too impoverished by war to be of much military use. The staunchly Lutheran city of Magdeburg was one of the few Protestant polities that dared to ally itself to Sweden. It paid dearly for its courage. While Gustavus negotiated with the Protestant princes, Tilly's Catholic forces sacked the defenseless city and murdered three-quarters of its inhabitants, some 30,000 men, women, and children.

Despite the uncertainty of the Protestant princes' support, the Swedish penetration into Germany was astonishingly rapid. The much-reduced imperial army, now under

This colored seventeenth-century engraving depicts the murder of Wallenstein in his bedroom in 1634 on the orders of the emperor Ferdinand.

A contemporary colored engraving shows the Battle of Lützen, between the Swedish army under Gustavus Adolphus and the imperial army under Wallenstein.

the command of Tilly, was no match for the Swedes' superior strength and discipline. When the two armies finally met at the Battle of Breitenfeld, on September 19, 1631, the imperial forces were soundly beaten, with the loss of some 2,000 men.

The Return of Wallenstein

The imperial army was in tatters, and the Swedes now held almost all of the northern part of the empire, from Mannheim on the Rhine to Prague in Bohemia. Protestant forces threatened the imperial capital, Vienna, itself.

In desperation, the emperor Ferdinand turned once again to Wallenstein, bribing him with the promise of new titles and privileges. Wallenstein immediately raised a new army and returned triumphantly to the field, rapidly regaining Bohemia for the empire. After a long game of cat and mouse, the armies of Gustavus Aldophus and Wallenstein finally met on November 16, 1632, at Lützen. Despite huge losses on both sides, neither army was able to gain the upper hand. Among the 15,000 left dead at the end of the fighting was the Swedish king himself. The Swedes fought on under the leadership of Gustavus's chief adviser, Axel Oxenstierna.

Wallenstein, meanwhile, was behaving in an increasingly erratic manner, taking it upon himself to begin his own negotiations with both the Swedes and the French. Whatever Wallenstein's real motives might have been, the emperor was sufficiently mistrustful to order his arrest in January

1634. The following month, Wallenstein was assassinated on the emperor's orders.

The decisive change to the war, however, came with the renewed intervention of the Spanish Habsburgs. Realizing that Protestant success in Germany would result in the eventual loss of the Spanish Netherlands, they rejoined the conflict.

The Peace of Prague

In July 1634, a Spanish army of some 15,000 men appeared in Germany and joined forces with the imperial army, which was now under the command of the emperor's son Ferdinand. Together, the two armies were able to deal a body blow to the Swedish and German Protestant forces at the Battle of Nördlingen on September 6. The imperial forces rapidly retook all of southern Germany.

This imperial victory and the subsequent Peace of Prague of 1635 initially seemed to settle the war in the empire's favor. Although no leniency would be extended to Frederick V or the Bohemian exiles, Ferdinand offered an amnesty to the other Protestant princes if they agreed to cease military opposition. There would also be, Ferdinand promised, an immediate repeal of the Edict of Restitution.

A European War in Germany

That the Peace of Prague did not bring open hostilities in Germany to an end is due primarily to the declaration of war by France on Spain in May 1635. This turn of events transformed the character of the

This painting by the Dutch painter Cornelisz Verbeek depicts the Battle of Downs of 1639, at which the Dutch fleet under Maarten Tromp defeated the Spanish fleet under Antonio de Oquendo.

Thirty Years' War. It meant that the war ceased—ostensibly, at least—to be about the religious freedoms of the Holy Roman Empire. Catholic France was now fighting Catholic Spain. France, which was ruthless in its campaign against its own domestic Protestants, the Huguenots, was prepared to support the Protestant cause, primarily as a means of thwarting the ambitions of its traditional enemy, Spain. The French saw their chance to achieve a long-term balance of power in Europe that would be far more in their favor.

Initially, therefore, the French campaigns in the German empire were concerned with preventing Ferdinand from aiding his Spanish cousins, and France declared war on the German emperor only in March 1636. For a long time, too, the Swedes did not feel that their war aims and those of the French were sufficiently close for them to work together as allies. Consequently, both the Swedes and French had little success during this period.

This seventeenth-century flask was used to keep a musketeer's gunpowder dry. Because the powder and ball were were still loaded from the end of the barrel, reloading was relatively slow.

The most damaging blows to the Habsburg cause at this time came from minor players in the Thirty Years' War. In 1639, the Dutch won a spectacular victory over the Spanish in the naval Battle of the Downs. The victory was to prove a decisive turning point in the young republic's struggle for full independence from the Spanish Habsburgs.

Not until it became clear that the Habsburgs could be defeated only by the force of numbers did France and Sweden at the Treaty of Hamburg in 1641 undertake a joint campaign. At the same time, the allies also agreed to take part in peace negotiations with the emperor in Westphalia. All parties, it seemed, were sick of the war and eager for peace.

While the peace talks continued, the new coalition proved strikingly successful on the battlefield. It defeated the imperial armies in a succession of battles—the Second Battle of Breitenfeld (November 1642), and the battles of Jankov (March 1645) and Allerheim (August 1645)—and as a consequence France and Sweden were able to negotiate ever more favorable concessions at the peace conference.

The Peace of Westphalia

The Peace of Westphalia of 1648 was the culmination of five years of negotiations among 194 rulers, great and small. It is one of the great landmarks of European history. Although the peace by no means solved all of the continent's problems, it created an effective balance of power that was to last well into the next century. Even a century later, French philosopher Jean-Jacques Rousseau could write of the peace, optimistically as it happened: "The Peace of Westphalia may well remain the foundation of our political system for ever."

Under the terms of the settlement, the power of the Holy Roman emperor was reduced, the German princes gained greater independence, and the Edict of Restitution was abandoned once and for all. Spain finally recognized the independence of the Dutch Republic. Meanwhile, Sweden was encouraged to rein in its territorial ambitions. France, however, proved harder to please. In the vain hope of bringing about the total collapse of the Habsburgs' power, it continued its war against Spain until 1659, when troubles at home made continuation of war impossible.

The elector of Saxony's copy of the Treaty of Münster: the formal document that accompanied the Peace of Westphalia of 1648.

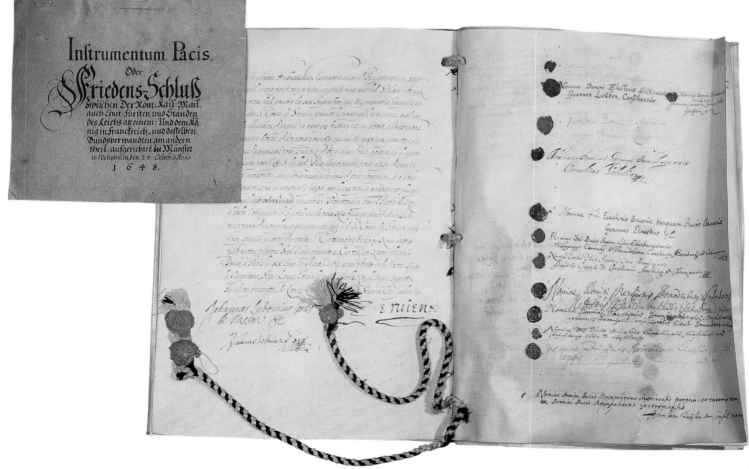

A nineteenth-century lithograph entitled *Camp Life in the Thirty Years' War* is a re-creation of what it might have been like to serve in one of the armies of the period. The camps housed not only the soldiers but numerous camp followers, including many women, who laundered and cooked for the fighting men.

The war and the concluding peace did more, however, than create a new map of Europe. After the treaty, the Protestant-Catholic divide ceased to be the major cause of conflict in international relations. As the character of the war changed and new alliances were formed that went beyond religious differences, the particular ambitions of an individual country became increasingly significant in determining the course of European history. The war marked the beginning of a period in which "reason of state" gained the upper hand. As one diplomat at the peace conference remarked: "Reason of state is a wonderful animal, it chases away all other reasons."

The new settlement was bought at a huge cost, however. For the civilian population of the Holy Roman Empire, the war had meant poverty, disruption, and the constant fear of assault and death at the hands of marauding troops. Armies destroyed crops and stole supplies, leaving people to go hungry. Statistics give an insight into the extent of the devastation. Contemporary censuses taken in the German duchy of Württemberg, for example, reveal that the population fell from 450,000 at the beginning of the war to only 166,000 at its end. Meanwhile, in the countryside, more than half of all houses were in ruins and a third of agricultural land was left uncultivated. In the heavy toll that it took on civilians, the Thirty Years' War was an ominous preview of the Napoleonic Wars and twentieth-century European wars.

England's Civil War

The Rise and Fall of the Stuart Dynasty

Early on January 30, 1649, King Charles I climbed onto a scaffold in London and knelt at the block. In front of a large crowd, an executioner cut off his head with an axe. The people of England had executed their king as a tyrant and traitor.

The execution marked the lowest point in the fortunes of the Stuart dynasty that ruled England for much of the seventeenth century. Charles led his country into a civil war from which England emerged as a republic. The Stuarts returned in 1660 and, after high and low fortunes, left England established as a parliamentary monarchy.

The first Stuart to rule England was James VI of Scotland, who became King James I of England in 1603 on the death of his cousin Elizabeth I (*see 2:205*). The accession of the thirty-six-year-old caused little controversy, a sign of the stability Elizabeth had brought to the throne. After James left Scotland for London, he returned to his native land only once.

King James I (1566–1625)

The new king was unprepossessing. He was scruffy and had a jaw so long and thin that he had difficulty eating and dribbled when he talked. James loved hunting, but he was an intellectual who felt more at home with scholarly works than with people. He had little contact with his subjects and was so tactless in expression that King Henry IV of France dubbed him "the wisest fool in Christendom."

Increasing Problems

With the help of his adviser Sir Robert Cecil, who had also served Queen Elizabeth, James set out to use his kingship as a

An artist's fanciful reconstruction shows King Charles I accompanied by a priest on his way to his execution in 1649. Despite his personal unpopularity, Charles's dignity in the face of death won him great sympathy and admiration.

A contemporary portrait shows James I in royal regalia. In fact, the king rarely appeared this smartly dressed. James was such a dedicated horseman that his English subjects blamed his thin legs on the fact that he rode everywhere.

reduce the power of the bishops who ran it, because he himself had been raised in a radical Scottish form of Protestantism, called Presbyterianism. James also came under pressure from England's Catholics, who had their own reasons to hope for a favorable response: James's mother had been the Catholic Mary, Queen of Scots, executed by the English in 1587.

Religious Strife

Early in his reign, at the 1604 Hampton Court Conference on doctrinal matters, James disappointed both parties. He refused Puritan requests to make the Church of England presbyterian rather than episcopalian, linking the bishops' authority to his own in the phrase, "No bishop, no king." James did, however, commission a new English translation of the Bible, completed by a team of scholars in 1611. Known as the King James Version, the Bible remains many people's favored translation.

While James involved Puritan scholars in the translation of the Bible, he ignored England's Catholics altogether. A group of disaffected Catholics sought revenge by plotting to kill the king. On November 5, 1605, Guy Fawkes was discovered in a cellar with barrels of gunpowder, preparing to blow up the king and both houses of Parliament. Fawkes and his fellow conspirators were hanged, drawn, and quartered. In England, November 5 is still celebrated each year as Guy Fawkes Night with bonfires and fireworks.

Decreasing Popularity

As James's reign went on, he grew less popular. The death of the Puritan sympathizer Robert Cecil in 1612 marked a turning point for the king. James turned to the company of two successive favorites, Robert Carr and George Villiers, both of whom had great influence on the king, who was almost certainly a homosexual. Villiers in particular, whom James made duke of Buckingham, disgusted the Puritans with his lifestyle.

Even many non-Puritans thought the king was too sympathetic to Catholic Spain. The Spanish ambassador persuaded James to execute Sir Walter Raleigh. The adventurer, who had been knighted by Elizabeth I, had attacked Spanish settlements in South America while searching for gold.

England's Puritans

Although they were only a minority of the population, England's Puritans had come to exercise great power in both church and Parliament. They had great influence on

tool for change. As king of England, Scotland, and Ireland, he wanted to unify the three countries into a single realm, but the English parliament refused. James believed that he could work with his fellow monarchs in Spain and France to bring harmony to Europe. Parliament, on the other hand, distrusted relationships with these Catholic powers.

James also believed that his position as head of the Church of England would help him resolve religious tensions at home; but in this, too, he was mistaken. Religious rifts underlay British politics, thanks to the parliamentary prominence of the Puritans, radical Protestant members of the Church of England. The Puritans wanted to change the church. They hoped that James would

public opinion through their sermons and writings, which circulated in the form of printed pamphlets and books. They resented the fact that the king lived in luxury and lavished gifts on his favorites while his subjects suffered from the effects of inflation and poor harvests. Parliament became even less well disposed to James when Buckingham and the king's son, Charles, slipped off secretly to Spain to arrange the prince's marriage to a daughter of the Catholic king Philip III. Thanks to Buckingham's arrogant behavior, the visit went so badly that England ended up declaring war on Spain.

King Charles I (1600–1649)

Working together, Charles and Buckingham gradually displaced James from effective power even before his death in 1625. Charles I was as unprepossessing as his father. He was frail, had a stammer, and was only a little over 5 feet tall. Shy and reserved, he lacked the popular touch. Soon after becoming king, he married a sister of the Catholic king of France, Louis XIII. The queen was hugely unpopular with her English subjects and earned Charles more distrust from the Protestant Parliament.

Parliament, meanwhile, also increasingly distrusted Buckingham. The Spanish war he had started was a failure. In 1627, Buckingham's clumsy diplomacy led to another war, this time with the French. Although a naval officer assassinated Buckingham in 1628, his influence had proved politically disastrous and financially expensive. While

the English people celebrated the assassination by dancing in the streets, the king wept in his palace.

Conflict with Parliament

Parliament had refused to fund Charles's military campaigns and forced him to increase parliamentary power. The Petition of Right established the principle that all taxes must be approved by Parliament. The next year, Parliament protested the king's raising of duties without its approval and his "popish practices," a reference to the king's contacts with Catholicism.

Charles ordered the speaker, John Finch, to dismiss Parliament. Members of Parliament responded by holding Finch down in his chair while they officially con-

The lantern used by Guy Fawkes in the cellars beneath the houses of Parliament, given to a nobleman as a souvenir in 1641.

A nineteenth-century painting re-creates the moment when Guy Fawkes was discovered beneath the houses of Parliament with tons of gunpowder.

demned the king's action. Charles determined never to hold another parliament.

Charles ruled without Parliament for eleven years. Inflation slowed and trade boomed. The king's title seemed secure, supported by advisers such as Sir Thomas Wentworth (1593–1641), later earl of Strafford, who became essentially the governor of northern England. A privy councillor, Wentworth dedicated his career to consolidating the power of the crown in an echo of the absolute monarchies of Europe. In 1633, Charles appointed Wentworth lord deputy of Ireland. Wentworth imposed a firm rule calculated to create a thriving Protestant Ireland that would be a valuable source of revenue to the English crown.

William Laud (1573–1645)

A religious crisis overtook Charles's reign. William Laud, who became archbishop of Canterbury in 1633, believed that rituals and priests were essential to religion and wanted to increase the power of England's bishops. To many people, this emphasis on the outward forms of religion seemed close to a return of Catholicism to England. Laud also believed in strict adherence to the Anglican prayer book. England's Puritans, on the other hand, only tolerated the prayer book because they traditionally ignored it in favor of their own observances. Laud, determined to enforce their adherence, launched a harsh campaign of persecution against the Puritans, many of whom fled, some to the New World.

In 1637, Charles attempted to impose on Scotland religious reforms similar to those Laud had achieved in England, including a new prayer book. The Scots rebelled, and Charles summoned Wentworth back from Ireland, ennobled him as the earl of Strafford, and sent him north to put down the rebellion. The Scots asserted their presbyterian religion and inflicted a humiliating defeat on Strafford. Scottish troops crossed the border and occupied the English city of Newcastle upon Tyne.

Toward Civil War

Short of money to fund a campaign against the Scots, Charles tried to raise a ship tax, supposedly for building up the navy. A leading Puritan member of Charles's last parliament, John Hampden, claimed that the tax was illegal. Although England's highest financial court disagreed, many people refused to pay. Charles recalled Parliament in 1640 to raise taxes. The so-called Short Parliament was reluctant to renew the fighting, however; a frustrated Charles dismissed it after only three weeks.

In November, threatened again by Scottish invasions, Charles summoned what became known as the Long Parliament. Parliament, supported by public opinion and strongly influenced by Puritan thinking, passed a number of laws to increase its own powers. It complained that royal policy was too influenced by Catholics, corrupt bishops, and foreign sympathizers.

King Charles reacted by ordering the arrest of five leading members of Parliament. Among them were John Hampden and John Pym, called "King Pym" because

This drawing shows a woman from the court of Charles I. The court was a glittering center of fashion where the king often staged elaborate costumed entertainments called masques.

The Arch-Prelate of St Andrewes in Scotland reading the new Service-booke in his pontificalibus assaulted by men & Women, with Cricketts stooles Stickes and Stones.

A contemporary engraving shows Scottish Presbyterians rioting in an Edinburgh cathedral in July 1637 as a priest reads from the new prayer book.

of his great influence in Parliament and in London. Charles himself led troops to the House of Commons to make the arrests, only to find that the five men had escaped.

As tension grew between the king and Parliament, Charles left the capital to tour northern England. Meanwhile, his wife went to Holland to raise funds for her husband by pawning the crown jewels. For its part, Parliament arrested Charles's advisers, including the earl of Strafford and William Laud, who were executed in 1641 and 1645, respectively.

The Lines Are Drawn

It did not seem that England would go to war, but clumsy maneuvers by both sides helped intensify the crisis. Charles offended many potential supporters when he made it clear that he would reverse the increases in Parliament's power as soon as he got the opportunity. John Pym, meanwhile, rallied aggressive crowds of apprentices onto the streets of London to urge Parliament to take a more radical stance against the king.

Meanwhile, as the Catholics of northern Ireland saw London's Protestant parliament increase its powers, they feared inevitable repression. To prevent this, they rose up and massacred some 3,000 Protestants in Ulster, one in five of the Protestant population. The massacre had repercussions in England. The Catholics had a false warrant that claimed that they were acting on the authority of the king. In the tense political atmosphere in England, it was easy for people to believe them.

The Drift to War

Pym attacked Charles as a lunatic unfit to rule, but other people were less personal in their reactions. Those who sided with either king or Parliament were usually more concerned with the future of the Church than with Charles or the monarchy. Many gentry, craftsmen, and farmers, for example, wanted to replace the Anglican Church with a more Puritan one. Others wanted to protect the Anglican religion from radical change.

The confrontation still involved only a minority of the population. The majority remained uninterested. As extremists on both sides hardened their stance, however, most people were forced to take sides, even if they had no strong feelings. Whole regions became Royalist or Parliamentarian. Hull, for example, a Puritan town in northern England, refused to admit the king in April 1640, when he tried to obtain an arsenal of military equipment stored there.

Both sides gathered forces. On August 20, 1642, Charles raised his standard, or flag, at Nottingham, formally declaring war. Both sides still expected not to fight— the opposing generals were often friends. People thought that negotiation or a single battle would end the conflict. When the first battle came, however, on October 23, 1642, at Edgehill on the way from Nottingham to London, it settled nothing.

The New Model Army

The Civil War falls into a transitional period in the history of warfare. Although combatants sometimes still wore full suits of

239

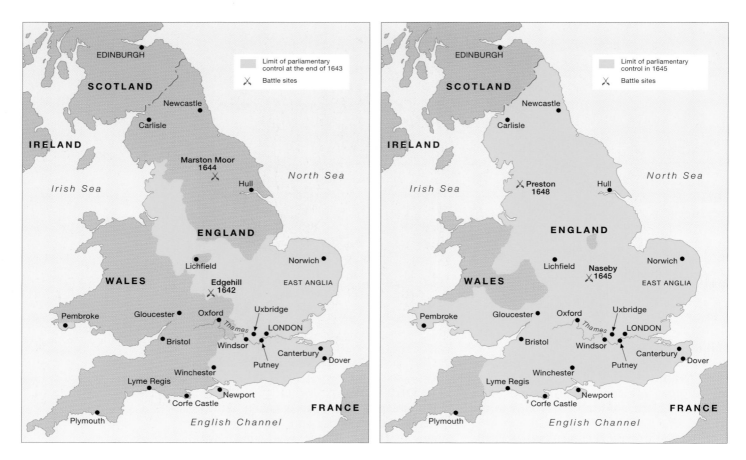

The yellow areas on the maps show how Parliament extended its control over England from 1643 (*left*) to 1645 (*right*).

armor designed to protect them against swords or pikes, guns were replacing the old edged weapons. At first, it was difficult for either side to win a decisive victory.

The first came in July 1644, when a combined Scottish and Parliamentarian army defeated the king at the Battle of Marston Moor. But the victors failed to follow through their advantage and force Charles to end the war.

In 1645, Parliament formed the so-called New Model Army, commanded by Sir Thomas Fairfax. Fairfax improved recruitment, organization, and training. He ensured that troops were well supplied and also that they were paid, which was not always the case for the Royalist forces. Fairfax and his general Oliver Cromwell—one of the outstanding tactical generals of English history—defeated the Royalists at the Battle of Naseby on June 14, 1645. Less than a year later, Charles surrendered to the Scots.

The Execution of the King

The Scots passed the king to the English, but in November 1647, he escaped back to Scotland, where he raised an army. When he crossed into England the next year, Charles was quickly defeated. Parliament put the king on trial for treason. A minority of radicals insisted that Charles receive the death penalty. More moderate members of

Charles I died, still claiming to be a martyr for his people, on a beheading block similar to this one, later used to execute English traitors at the Tower of London.

240

Parliament stayed away from the trial. In January 1649, the king was executed as a traitor. The king's dignity throughout his trial and as he faced death won him much sympathy. The execution stunned Europe.

Oliver Cromwell (1599–1658)

The Civil War had not ended, however. In Scotland, monarchists proclaimed Charles's son King Charles II and he led his rapidly assembled forces against the New Model Army. Within little over a year, however, he was defeated. After a dangerous forty days spent as a fugitive in England, hiding from enemy troops first in a tree and later in the homes of loyal monarchists, Charles escaped to the safety of France. The royalist cause was lost.

England became a republic, governed by Parliament, from whose ranks an outstanding leader soon emerged, Oliver Cromwell, commander of the New Model Army since 1650. A Puritan member of Parliament, Cromwell was a Civil War veteran with a reputation as a ruthless but outstanding general. He had led a bloody campaign to impose the rule of Parliament upon Ireland, culminating in the storming of Drogheda, near Dublin, in September 1649. Cromwell's troops massacred the town's inhabitants.

A More Radical Army

The New Model Army, meanwhile, had become more radical in its determination to impose Puritanism on England, even at the expense of its former allies in the war. The army had turned on Parliament itself in 1648 and purged, or driven out, those members whom it accused of being corrupt. In 1653, the army shut down Parliament by force of arms and declared Cromwell lord protector, or governor.

Although he was a staunch Puritan, Cromwell was not nearly so strict as some of his fellow religionists. He believed in toleration for others as long as they behaved peaceably; he fit poorly with the image of the Puritans as dour killjoys. He enjoyed music, hunting, smoking, drinking, and even dancing.

The Commonwealth

Although England was now a commonwealth, or an association for the common good, there were some ways in which little had changed. The aristocracy retained much power, for example. Cromwell was conservative in his social thinking, balancing the military power of the army with the social authority of the aristocracy. But he was also a religious radical who believed

that he was creating a society ordained by God, which he felt justified even unconstitutional behavior. He imprisoned people without trial and imposed military governors to improve morality.

Despite Cromwell's social conservatism, the Commonwealth was a hotbed of political and religious experimentation. So-called millenarian groups sprang up, convinced by signs and portents that Christ's second coming was imminent. Rather than establish a uniform Puritan Church in England, as many of the Parliamentarians had hoped, the aftermath of the war had the opposite effect. Religion fragmented as radical sects appeared, including the Seekers, Ranters, and Quakers.

The character of English life changed. Bible reading, praying, and fasting became popular at the expense of plays, dancing, and gambling. Such "ungodly" activities were suppressed. Puritan troops destroyed works of religious art. Puritanism was not necessarily in conflict with artistic achievement, however. Many artists and writers became Puritans. John Milton's epic poem *Paradise Lost* and John Bunyan's *Pilgrim's Progress* are both broadly Puritan creations that remain classics today.

The Restoration

Cromwell's forceful leadership kept him in power until his death in 1658, despite the fact that most of the country probably favored the restoration of the monarchy.

This woodcut showing the execution of Charles I comes from a contemporary broadside reporting the event.

These contemporary portraits of Oliver Cromwell and England's other military governors were published by monarchists under the heading, "Rebels, not Saints."

People offered Cromwell the crown, but he refused. After his death, his son Richard soon lost control of part of the army. The troops brought back the Long Parliament, which dissolved itself—eighteen years after it first sat—and called elections. The new Parliament offered the crown to Charles II. England's experiment with republicanism was over.

Charles arrived in London to popular rejoicing on his thirtieth birthday, May 25, 1660. He seemed unsure what to do with the throne he had always wanted. He was as interested in enjoying himself as in ruling the country, earning him the nickname of the Merry Monarch. Charles was a worldly man who spent money freely and fathered seventeen illegitimate children with a succession of mistresses. But he was also a mystic who believed that, as a divinely appointed king, he had the power to heal skin diseases by touch.

Some people point to Charles's cynical politics and immorality to show that he was as poor a monarch as the earlier Stuarts. Others see him in a more positive light, as a genial figure who at least brought tranquillity to the throne after the upheaval of the Civil War, the execution of his father, and Cromwell's rule.

A Moderate Settlement

Charles included both monarchists and moderate Puritans in his government, earning himself a reputation for political adaptability. Of those who had fought against the monarchy, he executed only the radicals who had actually signed his father's death warrant. Charles and his Parliament restored the Anglican Church. Charles remained thankful to England's Catholics, however, who had never abandoned his father. Most of the king's close family were Catholics, including his mother and his wife. Charles himself converted to Catholicism on his deathbed.

The king's efforts to win more religious toleration for Catholics, however, failed in the face of suspicion from his people and his Parliament. The House of Commons blocked his efforts to increase religious toleration. When the English fought the Dutch over trade, from 1665 to 1667, many people opposed fighting a fellow Protestant nation. They saw the Great Plague, which killed 75,000 Londoners in 1665, and the Great Fire of London, which destroyed four-fifths of the oldest part of the capital in 1666, as divine punishment. Charles suffered a humiliating defeat in 1667 when Dutch vessels sailed up the Medway to destroy English ships in harbors near London.

The Exclusion Crisis

The religious divide developed into a crisis in 1678. A dissenter called Titus Oates betrayed a plot by Catholics to kill the king and replace him with his Catholic brother, James, duke of York. Historians believe that the plot did not exist, but when an investigating magistrate died in suspicious circumstances, anti-Catholic hysteria swept England. Thirty-five alleged conspirators went to their deaths for their part in the supposed plot. Parliament revived vigorous anti-Catholic laws.

In 1679, Parliament considered a bill to exclude James from the throne. Determined to prevent its passing, Charles dissolved Parliament three times in two years. Each time a pro-exclusion Parliament was elected, Charles refused to accept it. He replaced England's local governors with his allies and held his nerve as his opponents lost theirs. In 1683, government agents

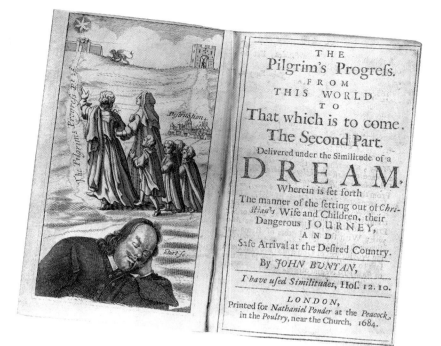

A first edition of part of John Bunyan's *Pilgrim's Progress.*

This print from 1689 shows William and Mary on the English throne. It illustrated a ballad called "The Protestants' Joy."

243

named the chief exclusionists as members of a conspiracy to assassinate the king. The accusation was probably untrue, but two of the accused were executed and the third killed himself. Charles had triumphed. When he failed to summon another Parliament, few objected. The king was at the height of his powers.

King James II (1633–1701)

When Charles died in 1685, the throne passed to his brother James II, despite an uprising by the Protestant duke of Monmouth, one of Charles's illegitimate sons. James had served as lord high admiral, promoting English interests in the New World. He had encouraged the seizure of New Amsterdam from the Dutch in 1664. The town was renamed New York in his honor.

As a Catholic, James sought toleration for his fellow believers. When he appointed Catholic officers to lead his army, however, Parliament protested. The king dismissed it and intensified his Catholic policy. In 1687, he suspended the laws against both Catholics and Protestant nonconformists.

In November 1687, an unexpected development galvanized opposition to James.

The fifty-year-old king's second wife was pregnant. When she successfully gave birth to a son the following June, England's Protestant majority faced the prospect of a long period of Catholic rule. Even James's supporters abandoned him. Many were nobles who were angry about a shake-up of local government, which lessened their social power.

The End of the Stuarts

England's Protestants invited the Dutch prince William of Orange, husband of James's Protestant daughter Mary, to bring troops to England to back them. William landed in England late in 1688. The king, meanwhile, suffered a breakdown. Hampered by incessant nosebleeds and losing his reason, the king lost the support of his army and fled to France in 1688. William came to the throne with his wife Mary.

In 1690, James arrived in Ireland to reclaim his throne with an army raised with French support. William defeated him at the Battle of the Boyne, a decisive encounter still celebrated by Irish Protestants. No Roman Catholic has since occupied the English throne.

Based on eyewitness accounts, a late-seventeenth-century painting shows the Great Fire of London raging through the city in 1666. In the background looms Old St. Paul's Cathedral, itself destroyed by the fire and rebuilt by the famous architect Sir Christopher Wren.

Everyday Life in Europe

Continuity and Change

For Europeans the seventeenth century was a time of both stability and change. In some ways they lived as their forebears had for generations. The majority of people still lived in villages and worked on the land, farming for themselves or for a local land-owner or lord. Fewer than one in ten of all Europeans lived in cities. The average life span remained relatively short. Few people survived even into their forties, killed by hunger, warfare, or disease.

In other ways, however, people's lives were changing. The Reformation (*see 2:151*) changed ideas about religion. Printing led to an increased circulation of ideas. Overseas trade grew and the economy became more complex.

At the heart of the change lay population growth and fall. In the fourteenth century, Europe's population plummeted as a result of a plague called the Black Death. In 1347, rats with plague-carrying fleas had arrived in Italy on merchant ships. Within a year, the disease had spread as far as Scandinavia. By the time the plague ended, between one-third and one-half of Europe's population had died. By the sixteenth century, however, population numbers had recovered (*see 1:29*). Europe had more people than it needed to work the land. In

The Peasant Wedding, painted by Pieter Brueghel the Elder about 1565, shows peasants at a celebratory feast in northern Europe. Two waiters carry bowls of plain-looking food on a tray made from a door, while on the left another prepares jugs of beer for the revelers.

245

Iron shears like these were used to remove sheep's fleeces. The heavy work of shearing was usually undertaken by men.

nary people, farmed the land of a minority, the lords, to whom the people owed a proportion of their labor and produce. In return, the most powerful members of society had a duty to protect the weakest.

This social organization, which people believed was ordained by God, was called the body politic. Like the parts of the human body, each member of society had a particular role: no member could perform the role of another, any more than the feet could think or the brain digest. Everyone fit his or her own particular role, otherwise a community would not function properly. In the proper order of things, neighbors cooperated in work, entertainment, and worship. Peer pressure made sure that everyone conformed and stayed in place.

Radical Thinking

Economic developments put great pressure on traditional roles, and the traditional view of society became more difficult to sustain. As the European cloth market expanded, for example, many landowners switched from growing grains and began raising sheep to supply the demand for wool. In doing so, however, they often had to enclose, or build fences around, fields that had traditionally been used by their villagers to grow crops. Deprived of their right to use the land, the villagers lost the ability to feed themselves. Enclosure caused such hunger and hardship that the sixteenth-century English politician Sir Thomas More commented: "Sheep, which are usually so tame and cheaply fed, begin now... to be so greedy and wild that they devour human beings."

Such an upheaval in the pattern of life gave villagers more cause to question the landowner's role in the proper order of things. The concept of the body politic also had no explanation for the increasing numbers of unemployed. If everyone had his or her role in society, what place did someone without a job have? The existence of people who did not fit into the community questioned the ideas of social organization.

Religious Challenges

Some challenges to the social order were inspired by religion. The Reformation had weakened the moral authority of the Catholic Church. This development unleashed social forces such as the 1525 peasant revolt in Germany (*see 2:156*). Sects such as the Arminians rejected the whole idea of the body politic. They refused to acknowledge any earthly authority but answered to God alone. Other groups used the Bible as a basis to call for political change.

the next century, the population leveled off. It actually fell in the latter half of the century, for reasons historians are still debating. Some argue that poor weather and bad harvests in the middle of the century had the effect of increasing mortality rates.

Rural communities that had been static for generations changed as people left. Some drifted to towns to look for work; some emigrated to the New World; others joined the mercenary armies that fought in Europe's almost constant wars. New problems emerged, such as unemployment and rising prices, which were caused by shortages of goods. The impact of such changes led to division and conflict. Some people began to question the very organization of the society in which they lived.

The Proper Order

The organization of society was based on an order that had long been accepted as natural and unchanging. The majority, ordi-

Such ideas were frightening to people in power. They appealed to many others, however, who felt discontented with their lot. Throughout Europe, peasants rebelled to improve their conditions. Some towns claimed the right to govern themselves. Political movements tried to harness the dissatisfaction. In England, for example, the Levellers called for the establishment of a republic, while the Diggers wanted to abolish all private property. In 1649, when the English executed their king (*see 2:235*), it seemed that the natural order of things had been turned upside down.

A Range of Experiences

Some Europeans lived increasingly varied lives. There were major differences between the rich and the poor, merchants and aristocrats, men and women. For hundreds of years, citizens of Venice had rubbed shoulders with traders from Africa and the Middle East. Peasant farmers from Russia or France, on the other hand, met few strangers in their lives and never traveled farther than the nearest market.

Contact with Nature

All seventeenth-century Europeans lived in close synchronization with the cycles of nature. Farmers' lives were ruled by the weather. The patterns of work, idleness, prosperity, and dearth that defined rural life were determined by the seasons and the fickleness of sun, rain, and wind.

Nature dominated human activity. People could travel overland only when the roads were not choked with mud, sail only when rivers were not frozen or in flood, and eat only what was in season. Most people relied on natural light. Although people used oil lamps and tallow candles to light their homes, they were often very smoky. Even in cities, most work was done while the sun was up. In most towns and cities in Europe, it was against the law to be on the street after dark. Civic governors believed that anyone out at night must be up to no good.

Disease and Medicine

The lives of most Europeans were shaped by the need to survive. Inadequate diet, poor housing, and lack of sanitation meant that disease was rife. Only one in every four children born to French peasants survived infancy, for example. Before the invention of vaccinations, children and adults were at constant risk from potentially fatal illnesses such as influenza, typhus, typhoid, and smallpox.

Disease often spread in epidemics that killed large numbers of people in an area.

Plague killed 150,000 Londoners in the seventeenth century. Carried by fleas on rats, the disease spread rapidly. The only sure way to escape was to flee. The English court and nobles left the city. The poor found it more difficult to move. To keep the disease away, some provincial towns erected gallows to hang anyone from London who tried to enter.

There were few hospitals. Doctors studied the theories of the Roman physician Galen, who believed that the body was

One of a series of sixteenth-century miniatures illustrating the tasks associated with the months of the year, *July* shows sheepshearing. The countryside has been enclosed and is broken up by fences to stop sheep from wandering.

This early-seventeenth-century decorated plate shows people sowing crops in the fields. The annual harvest was the most important event in a village's year. Its success guaranteed the community's survival.

made up of four "humors": earth, air, fire, and water. Sickness resulted when the humors were out of balance. By examining the patient's urine or consulting astrological charts, the doctor would decide how to balance the humors. He might attach leeches, sluglike creatures that sucked the blood, or pray for divine assistance.

Such treatment was expensive. The poor relied on other, possibly more reliable, specialists. Every community had at least one midwife, for example, who assisted at births. Although midwives lacked any formal medical training, their experience and their familiarity with medicinal herbs more than made up for this disadvantage. Doctors often went to midwives for advice.

Diet and Nutrition

People were in greater danger of disease when they were weakened by malnutrition due to food shortages. Famines were not as common as in previous centuries, however.

Toward the end of the seventeenth century, they became less frequent still as it became easier to transport food such as grain around Europe and as fishermen found rich new fisheries in the Atlantic (*see 3:387*).

For most of the century, however, the danger of starvation was rarely far from the mind of the average person. Farming relied heavily on the weather, and food could easily run short if there was a bad harvest. Famine also struck when warring armies swept across a region, destroying crops and pillaging livestock and stores of food. People might have to eat acorns or bark or even, in desperate times, resort to cannibalism. A French doctor observed in 1660: "The famine is so great that the peasants go without bread and throw themselves onto carrion. As soon as a horse or other animal dies, they eat it."

When there was enough to eat, meals were often monotonous. The diet was low in fat, since meat was reserved almost

248

exclusively for special occasions, such as religious feasts. There were few ways to preserve food, so people usually ate whatever was freshest. Meals changed according to the season. Most people ate an endless round of hard bread, gruel, cheese, and boiled vegetables. The most popular drinks were beer, made from fermented hops, and wine, made from fermented grapes. Water usually came from a river or stream or from a well. Although many people thought it unhealthy to drink water, water sellers carrying huge jugs through the city streets were a common sight.

Sanitation and Living Conditions

The risk of disease was increased by poor sanitation. Few urban apartments had bathrooms. Most people emptied their chamber pots into the street. Few homes had bathtubs, and civic authorities had closed many bathhouses. People thought that communal bathing spread disease and encouraged immorality. Soap—either hard soap made with soda or liquid soap made with potash—

A manuscript illustration from about 1482 shows the four Virtues in black visiting the nuns who run a hospital. Medical care was basic in such charitable hospitals: the patients had to share beds.

This early-seventeenth-century set of knives has carved-ivory handles, which mark it as a valuable luxury. Knives were the main implements used at the dinner table. The fork had recently become widely used in Italy and Spain, but its adoption throughout the rest of Europe was slow.

This wooden board hung outside a school in Germany during the first half of the sixteenth century. It shows both a man and a woman teaching children to read and write. There are no desks, only lecterns and benches.

was scarce and mainly used for laundry. A popular saying claimed that a person only ever needed two baths: one at baptism and the other in preparation for burial.

Other living conditions were also basic. Rural housing generally offered only partial protection from the elements. Houses were one- or two-story structures made of wood or wood and mud, with thatched or tiled roofs and dirt floors. Because glass was expensive, windows were generally small, so houses were dark. Rooms and furniture were painted bright colors to create the impression of light. Not all homes had glass in the windows: some used oiled paper, and some window frames were open. The average person lived in one or two rooms with his or her family and, occasionally, their livestock. The same space functioned as living room, bedroom, and kitchen, and sometimes also as a workshop.

Different Lifestyles

Privacy was a luxury that only the rich could enjoy. Their houses were usually larger and built of more durable materials such as stone and brick. By modern standards, however, such homes were not very comfortable. The large stone or brick fireplace that formed the focal point of many rooms was often inadequate. At the end of the seventeenth century, an observer at the French royal palace of Versailles—one of the grandest buildings in Europe—recorded how, in one cold December, "At the King's table the wine and water froze in the glass." In poorer homes, people crowded around the kitchen hearth for warmth.

Furniture and Fashions

The vast majority of Europeans owned relatively little in the way of furniture or clothing. The poor slept on bundles of straw, while the better-off had hard, wooden four-poster beds. For a poor family, the most important possessions were probably

This engraving of a kitchen is taken from one of the earliest cookbooks, printed in Italy about 1585. The furniture and equipment are very basic, as was most of the food people ate at the time. On the right, a man churns milk to make butter or cheese.

250

the cooking pans. Sitting on benches or stools, people ate at long, narrow tables or at planks resting on top of barrels. In winter, they all faced the fire to share its heat.

Peasants tended to dress in traditional clothes made of coarse, homespun cloth. Most of them kept their brighter and better outfits for going to church or the tavern on Sundays and for feast days. Their shoes consisted of soles tied onto the bottom of the feet with straps wrapped around the ankles. New clothes were a rare treat. One peasant's will left money for his widow to buy "One pair of shoes and a chemise [shirt] every two years and a dress of coarse cloth every three."

Among the richer classes, however, it became a matter of status to keep up with changing fashions. At one time, for example, aristocrats and well-off merchants adopted all-black costumes inspired by the Spanish. There were also many intricate variations of the great collars called ruffs, as there were in the hairstyles of both women and men.

Marriage of Convenience

The lives of rich and poor varied greatly when it came to marriage. For the sons and daughters of the wealthy, the choice of partner was, more often than not, made for them. Marriages among the elite had less to do with love than with political and economic alliances between powerful or wealthy families. These pairings tended to be made while the children were young. Children could be betrothed while they were still infants.

People lower down the social ladder, in contrast, tended to marry more on emotional grounds. In the main, they still married people from a similar class and background. They also tended to marry relatively late, in their mid to late twenties, as it was accepted that a husband needed to have achieved a level of financial independence in order to support a family. Because people often died young, marriages tended not to last very long. Women tended to die younger than men, mainly due to complications in childbirth, so some men remarried two or three times.

A Skimmington Party

Within marriage, as within society, there was a natural order of things. In particular, people believed that the husband should take the dominant role in a marriage. If he did not, then the community would show its disapproval in a variation of what was known in Britain as a Skimmington party. The villagers would ride by the house of

the offending couple in the middle of the night. They would play loud and discordant music and ride backward on their horses and mules, the men dressed as women, the women dressed as men. All of these things conveyed the message that the couple had upset the proper order of things. They would only be accepted as respectable members of the community again when the "natural" order was restored.

Community Ties

Such displays of peer-group pressure were an important means of maintaining communal discipline and conformity. Early communities had no police forces, so villagers largely policed themselves. Life then

Jan van Eyck's 1434 portrait, known as the *Arnolfini Marriage*, is full of symbols of hope for the union. The little dog, for example, is a symbol of fidelity, while the one candle burning in the chandelier stands for the all-seeing eye of God.

251

tended to be far more public than life today, and the community interfered in matters that would now be considered personal, such as relationships within families. The closeness of neighborly ties was reflected in people's vocabulary. Where we might use the word *associate*, seventeenth-century Europeans used the word *friend*. Where we might use the word *friend*, they used the word *lover*. Such use of language suggests an intimate and supportive society. The downside of such a society, however, was that relationships between people were so close that no individual's private life was truly private.

Trades and Apprenticeships

Despite the dominance of agriculture, not everyone became a farmer. There were many other trades, though some, such as brewing, were closely related to agriculture. In the city, for example, young boys often became apprentices in the shops of master craftsmen. There, over a period of seven or more years, they would learn a trade, such as carpentry or stone masonry. Other children devoted themselves to the formal education that might lead to a career in law, medicine, or the church. Their long hours in school were spent memorizing the content and imitating the style of the great books of the ancient world. All "educated" people could speak and write Latin, partly because it was the language of the Catholic Church and partly because the Humanists of the Renaissance established its primacy as the language of "serious" communication.

A sixteenth-century engraving shows a printer's workshop in the Netherlands. In the foreground, a man arranges movable type to create a page of text.

A painting of Venice shows the irregular layout of the streets. An increase of wheeled traffic during the sixteenth century saw other European towns try to regularize their street plans.

Life in the Cities

The sixteenth century was a time of great expansion for Europe's towns and cities. A region such as Flanders supported a high concentration of smaller towns, while individual cities grew at a remarkable pace. Amsterdam's population grew from 30,000 in 1530 to 115,000 in 1630. By the century's end, Europe's largest city, London, had 250,000 inhabitants.

The rise in the urban population reflected economic developments. Towns were the hubs of a trading network that covered Europe and beyond. Merchants built exchanges and banks to conduct their business. Master craftsmen formed guilds to control their trade. Doctors, architects, artists, and engineers served the needs of the town's better-off citizens.

The towns' wealth also attracted vast numbers of the poor. Some were peasants evicted from their fields by enclosure. They became shoemakers, masons, hawkers, or beggars. Often they lived in little more than hovels in the town's suburbs. In crowded cities, such as London, they made their home in a warren of tiny, dirty backstreets. In other places, they might find

A detail from a mid-seventeenth-century painting by Jan Vermeer shows a street in the Dutch city of Delft. Dutch towns prided themselves on their cleanliness, which was made possible partly by efficient water supplies based on their canals.

accommodation in buildings that could reach as high as ten stories.

The towns were still closely linked with the countryside, despite the protective walls that ringed most European centers. Many urban inhabitants left the town during harvest time to work in the fields. In 1540, for example, pirates were able to sack the town of Gibraltar in Spain because the inhabitants were all at the grape harvest. Towns had gardens, orchards, and fields inside and outside the walls. People raised pigs in the town streets.

The pigs only added to the town's dirt. Streets were often so muddy that they had to be crossed on stilts. People going visiting had to carry a spare pair of shoes to put on when they arrived. The raised sidewalks, reserved for the nobility, could also be dangerous as householders still emptied their chamber pots out of upstairs windows. A traveler in Madrid described how the streets were washed down with barrels of water: "It often happens that one encounters torrents of this evil water which blocks one's way and poisons by its stench." One visitor to Paris claimed that the smell made it impossible to stay there.

As towns became more crowded, the narrow streets became blocked with innu-

merable wagons carrying firewood or produce. A Londoner complained that "In every street carts and coaches make such a thundering as if the world ran on wheels." At the end of the century, some cities, such as Rome, began to build larger, straighter streets to cope with the growing number of horse-drawn coaches.

A painting from about 1530 shows a cloth market in a Dutch town. Towns were the natural centers for increasing European trade.

This pair of stocks still stands on a village green near Oxford in England. Offenders were placed in the stocks as a punishment for minor crimes. Most societies in early modern Europe placed a high value on public humiliation as a deterrent from offenses against the community.

Increasing Literacy

Other, less formal kinds of education touched a wider range of the population (*see 1:54*). The early modern world increasingly relied on the written word, and more people learned to read and write. Some needed to be literate for their jobs. Traders, for example, needed to understand bills of exchange, which acted as banknotes in long-distance trade, while seamen needed to read maps and charts. The emphasis placed on Bible study by Protestantism also encouraged the growth of literacy. Political groups, such as the Levellers, relied on pamphlets to spread ideas. In the cities, where literacy was particularly important to economic success, male literacy climbed to nearly 50 percent by the end of the sixteenth century. In Europe as a whole, however, literate people remained a minority.

Books Everywhere

The increased numbers of literate people went hand in hand with an increase in reading material, thanks to technological developments. Paper had been made in Europe since the thirteenth century: new techniques made it cheaper to make. In the mid-fifteenth century, Johannes Gutenberg invented the printing press (*see 1:59*).

In the Middle Ages, books were rare and expensive. Each copy of a manuscript required countless hours of effort by a scribe, usually a monk, who wrote it out by hand. Books were written on vellum, made from expensive sheepskin. To create a single copy of the Bible required the skins of some two hundred sheep.

Printing allowed a dramatic expansion in the number and range of books. There were books for every taste and every kind of reader, including picture books for children and adults who were not good at reading. People could read about everything from religious debates to an account of the birth of a miraculous two-headed pig in London. Such an unnatural event was taken as a portent of momentous events.

Shrinking Europe

As the economy expanded and communities became more interconnected and interdependent, Europeans became more aware of the world beyond their immediate surroundings. People began to realize that, as much as they identified with their community, they belonged to larger groupings, too. They were French, English, or Spanish, Protestant or Catholic.

New markets also prompted the large-scale migration of people seeking work, moving from one region to another or from the country to the city. It became less common to grow up in the same village as one's forebears had. The traditional village had a counterpart in communities of shifting populations whose inhabitants might not share the same customs or religion.

In the long run, Europeans would forge new bonds and a new sense of community based on the idea of the nation. The process was frightening for many people, however. Even as their daily lives continued much as they always had, the old certainties of life were disappearing.

The Baroque World

Energy and Emotion

By the early seventeenth century, the rift between the Catholic and Protestant churches had transformed the arts. Both the kinds of painting, sculpture, and architecture people produced and the kinds of people who commissioned them had changed.

Changes in styles, subject matter, and patronage largely followed the nature of the religions themselves. The art of Catholic countries such as Italy and Spain was able to grow directly out of the traditions of the High Renaissance (*see 1:79*). It was as complex, dramatic, and emotional as Catholic ritual itself.

The art of Protestant countries, on the other hand, defined itself largely against the heritage of Catholic art. While Protestant artists were able to build on the achievements of the Northern Renaissance —the art of such figures as Dürer and Cranach—Protestant iconoclasm, or opposition to religious imagery, meant that they had to look for both new subject matter and new patrons.

The World of the Senses

Despite such differences, it is possible in retrospect to see unifying themes that bind together much seventeenth-century art. It is with such hindsight that art historians sometimes label the century's art "baroque." The origins of the term are obscure, but some scholars derive it from the old Portuguese word *barrocco*, meaning a deformed pearl.

One unifying theme that runs through much seventeenth-century art, whether Catholic or Protestant, is its engagement with the world of the senses. Broadly speaking, the art of the Renaissance sought for intellectual and formal ideals of harmony; that of the Baroque age, by contrast, appealed to the senses—to the pleasures of color, pattern, and illusory effects—and, through these, to the emotions. More than ever before, paintings, sculptures, and buildings required the viewer to respond in a sensuous, even physical, way.

This deepening engagement with the world of the senses led in two apparently contradictory directions. In the first place, there was a new tendency toward grandeur and extravagance. Church domes, richly gilded and decorated with swirling painted figures, pulled the viewer up to the heavens. Huge palaces were imposing

The Italian artist Annibale Carracci's ceiling frescoes for the Palazzo Farnese in Rome, painted in 1597–1600, were the first masterpieces of the Baroque. In this corner section, it is difficult to tell where architectural decoration ends and painted ceiling begins. Such illusionistic effects are one of the hallmarks of the Baroque style.

255

reminders of the wealth and power of the absolute monarchs who lived within them. In painting and sculpture, compositions were often dramatic and full of movement; the colors were rich and stimulating. Painters and sculptors sometimes deliberately strove to deceive the viewer and to blur the boundaries between art and life. At court, lavish entertainments blended theater, dance, and opera in "multimedia" events that stimulated all the senses.

At the same time, however, the Baroque's engagement with the world of the senses also implied a closer inspection of reality. This change paralleled and sometimes fed on the development of empirical science, in which the patient observation of natural phenomena led to scientific truths about the physical world (*see 2:265*). In the light of such discoveries, many seventeenth-century artists began to show a deepening interest in the world around them and in everyday experience.

This new naturalism in art led artists to portray people as individuals rather than types, to depict the intimate spaces of domestic life, and to paint "still lifes"—pictures that depicted things rather than people—that rendered such natural phenomena as flowers, fruit, vegetables, and seashells with scientific exactitude.

In this version of *Judith Slaying Holofernes*, painted in 1612 or 1613, artist Artemisia Gentileschi chillingly portrays the strength and determination of the biblical heroine. These depictions differ greatly from the voluptuous nudes more usually found in the art of this period—for example, in the work of the Carracci brothers.

In the Italian painter Caravaggio's *Supper at Emmaus* (1596–1598), Christ's appearance to the apostles takes place during an ordinary meal: the apostle on the right, for instance, still has a twisted napkin in his lap. For his contemporaries, Caravaggio's art brought the biblical stories startlingly to life.

256

The Art of Persuasion

For the Catholic Church, art and architecture had an important ideological role to play. They were powerful means by which the church could spread its message of a renewed and vigorous faith that was still, despite the claims of Protestantism, the "one and true Church."

What was needed, the church saw, was an art that could make a direct and emotional appeal to the average churchgoer. It found an intellectual basis for this point of view in the work of the sixteenth-century Catholic reformer Saint Ignatius Loyola (1491–1556), who argued that it was through the senses rather than the intellect that the individual most easily attained spiritual understanding (*see 2:170*).

The Baroque style that found its first expression in the Italy of the turn of the century but that quickly spread to other parts of Catholic Europe was in large part a response to this call from the Catholic hierarchy for a more emotional, sometimes confrontational, type of art. Art was to be a kind of visual sermon to the faithful, a bulwark of belief.

The Art of the Catholic Baroque

At the end of the sixteenth century, the Catholic Church undertook an extensive building campaign in Rome, in part in response to the demands of the Catholic revival. The churches of the Gothic and Renaissance periods had often been vast and cavernous, and the long nave and aisles had distanced the faithful from the altar. The new Baroque churches, while retaining the awe and drama of the older buildings, were generally much smaller, intimate places that brought clergy and people both physically and emotionally closer together.

The Church of San Carlo alle Quattro Fontane, in Rome, built by the Italian architect Francesco Borromini (1599–1667) from 1638 to 1641, is a good example of this new style. Its unusual oval ground plan enabled worshipers to see the altar, while an elaborate interior structure added to the sense of enveloping intimacy.

A similar emphasis on intimacy and emotion is apparent in the painting and sculpture of the Catholic Baroque. This new movement in art found one of its first great exponents in the painting of Michelangelo da Merisi (1573–1610). Caravaggio, as da Merisi is generally known, is one of the more colorful figures in the history of art. His violent temper brought him into frequent conflict with the law—he once killed a man in an argument over a disputed score in a tennis match and

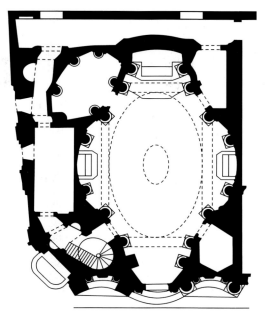

This ground plan of Francesco Borromini's San Carlo alle Quattro Fontane, in Rome, shows the elaborate play of spatial forms that helped create a sense of intimacy new to Catholic architecture in Italy.

Peter Paul Rubens's 1612 painting of *The Deposition* (or *Descent from the Cross*) sets naturalistic detail, such as the old man at the top who holds the shroud between his teeth, in a robust "corkscrew" composition. A committed Catholic, Rubens brought the art of the Italian Counter-Reformation to the Habsburg court of the Spanish Netherlands.

257

The Italian sculptor and architect Gianlorenzo Bernini's sculpture of Saint Teresa of Ávila forms the centerpiece of his Cornaro Chapel (1645–1652) in the church of Santa Maria della Vittoria, in Rome. Bernini wanted to express the unity of the Catholic Church by combining architecture, sculpture, and decoration into what was called *un bel composto*—"a beautiful whole."

was forced to flee Rome as a consequence. His paintings, too, show an earthy realism that was entirely new to religious art.

In his work, Caravaggio tried to make the biblical stories more human and immediate. His *Supper at Emmaus*, for example, depicts the moment when Christ first makes himself known to his disciples after the Crucifixion. The disciples are shown as ordinary, weather-beaten men—only the figure of Jesus is given a measure of otherworldliness as a reflection of his divinity. Caravaggio heightens the drama and emotions of the moment by his use of a technique called chiaroscuro—Italian for "light-dark"—in which abrupt divisions of light and shade are used to highlight the expressions and gestures of the figures.

Extreme Emotions

Caravaggio's influence on the art of the seventeenth century was immense. Artists everywhere copied his techniques. One such artist was Artemisia Gentileschi (1593–1653). Women artists were rare, in general because few women had the opportunity to play any public role and in particular because female artists did not have access to the painting academies that began to be set up in this period. Gentileschi was fortunate in that her father, Orazio Gentileschi, was a successful artist himself and was able to teach her.

Gentileschi was able to forge her own recognizably personal style, often using it to portray powerful women from the Old Testament. A theme to which she returned again and again was the story of Judith, in which the heroine decapitates the commander of an attacking army. In her paintings, Gentileschi unusually uses the female form to express, not sexual charm, but an energy and strength of expression generally associated with men.

The sculptor Gianlorenzo Bernini (1598–1680), who also worked as an architect, also portrayed extreme states of emotion. His masterpiece is perhaps the *Altar of St. Teresa*, made from 1645 to 1652 as the centerpiece of a chapel he designed in Rome. Saint Teresa of Ávila (1515–1622) was an important figure in the Counter-Reformation. This religious reformer's spiritual autobiography, *Life of the*

Mother Teresa of Jesus, promoted an extremely mystical and highly emotional brand of Catholicism. Bernini's sculpture illustrates a particular passage from her book, in which she describes how an angel appeared to her and pierced her side with a flaming arrow: "The pain was so great that I screamed; but at the same time I felt such an immense sweetness that I wanted the pain to last for ever."

In his *Water Carrier of Seville,* painted around 1619, the Spanish artist Velásquez depicts with sympathy the everyday life of ordinary people. Velásquez's work also included a series of realistic, even unflattering, portraits of the Habsburg royal family.

259

The Spread of the Catholic Baroque

The Baroque style was essentially forged in Italy, especially in Rome, which was the seat of the papacy. From here, however, the style rapidly spread throughout Catholic Europe. In Spain, Diego de Velásquez (1599–1660), like Caravaggio, showed an acute interest in depicting the lives of ordinary people. This realism is evident, for example, in his *Water Carrier of Seville*, in which he gives the old water carrier handing water to a thirsty boy the dignity of a priest giving wine at Catholic Communion.

Velásquez, who in 1623 became court painter to the Spanish king Philip IV, also painted many portraits of church digni-taries. His portrait of Pope Innocent X, for example, gives a powerful impression of the church leader. The pyramidlike composition made by the pope's body suggests all the solid foundations of a Catholic Church that intended to endure.

The Flemish, Spanish-ruled part of the Netherlands, centered on the flourishing port of Antwerp, also produced its own contribution to the art of the Catholic Baroque. The Antwerp-born painter Peter Paul Rubens (1577–1640) spent eight years in Italy, during which he mastered the new Italian style and deepened his sympathy for the Catholic religion. Rubens always managed to imbue his paintings with deeply felt

The clock tower of the Westerkerk in Amsterdam, designed by Hendrik de Keyser, is an example of the Protestant Baroque style of architecture.

emotion. His *Descent from the Cross* of 1612, painted as part of a triptych, or three-part altarpiece, for Antwerp Cathedral is—with its rich, strong colors and dramatic composition, or arrangement of figures—one of the most harrowing depictions of the Crucifixion in Western art.

Protestant Baroque

Just as the Counter-Reformation helped create a new style of Catholic art, so the rise of Protestantism brought about its own transformation of artistic practice.

A central part of the Protestant quarrel with the Catholic Church was what it considered the latter's idolatrous worship of religious images, such as the Madonna and Child or painted crucifixes. The Protestant faith emphasized the importance of teaching from the Bible. The new Protestant churches were an expression of this more austere, book-based faith. Dutch churches in country towns, for example, were often simple assembly halls. Their sole ornament might consist of the dark, carved wood of the simple pews, pulpit, and organ loft. Even the grandest of city churches emphasized simplicity in their structure and decoration. The Dutch architect Hendrik de Keyser (1565–1621) created what became the prototype for a Reformed church when he built the Westerkerk in Amsterdam. The church's central plan enabled all the faithful to gather about the pulpit to listen to the Word of God.

Because Protestant artists were no longer asked to produce the elaborate church decorations and altarpieces found in Catholic churches, they had to seek a new clientele for their work. They found a ready market in the middle classes, which consisted largely of merchants made wealthy by the development of trade through the sixteenth century. Holland, or the United Provinces, was a rich, independent country known as the "republic of merchants" for its many businessmen (*see 2:222*). Holland was an important market for secular, or nonreligious, artworks. For the wealthy Dutch merchants, paintings were a new commodity to be bought, sold, and admired.

The Art of the Everyday

The new middle class wanted an art that reflected its own interests and concerns. So instead of the grand, elaborate mythological and historical paintings favored by aristocratic patrons, a new art developed that emphasized the everyday life, experience, and values of ordinary people.

Sometimes such scenes resembled the moralizing sermons that could be heard in

the Protestant churches. Flemish-born artist Adriaen Brouwer (c. 1605–1638), for example, painted low-life scenes in which artisans were shown drunk and disorderly and held up as examples of how *not* to live life.

Sometimes, however, an artist would show just the kind of modest and simple lifestyle that good Protestants were supposed to live. The Dutch painter Pieter de Hooch (1629–1684), for example, painted serene pictures of well-ordered houses and courtyards, in which the inhabitants—often mothers and their children—go soberly about their business. Later in his life, Dutch artist Frans Hals (c. 1581–1666) painted group portraits of unsmiling regents and regentesses, the benefactors responsible for the maintenance of the many charitable institutions, such as homes for the poor or elderly, set up in the Dutch Republic during this period.

Sometimes, too, painters depicted the commodities that were the bread and butter of merchants' livelihoods. Still lifes, for example, might show the rare species of tulips that were bought and sold at inflated prices in Amsterdam's flower markets or

In this painting, called *The Art of Painting* (c. 1665), the Dutch artist Jan Vermeer depicts an artist, possibly himself, painting a model dressed as Clio, the muse of history. Vermeer's paintings are full of the colors and textures of everyday things: rich materials, black-and-white-tiled floors, burnished metal. On the wall behind is a contemporary map of the Dutch Republic.

Nicolas Poussin, *Landscape with a Man Bitten by a Snake* (c. 1648). Poussin (1594–1665) was one of the great painters of seventeenth-century France. He painted many landscapes. Landscape was a relatively new subject matter for painting at this time. Previously, artists had largely used it as an idealized backdrop for mythological or biblical stories.

the beautiful seashells that were highly prized by collectors. Domestic scenes might feature the rich tapestries that were made in nearby Flanders.

The emphasis on domestic, or so-called genre, scenes and still life in Protestant art enabled many more women to participate in artistic production. Rachel Ruysch (1664–1750), for example, specialized in intricate and botanically exact flower-pieces, while Judith Leyster gave a rare

French Baroque: Art and Power

In France, the monarchy, rather than the Catholic Church, exerted the most influence on the development of the arts. As a consequence, French art produced a quite distinctive reaction to the Italian Baroque, introducing a powerful strain of classicism.

Louis XIV (1638–1715; *see 4:449*) was the first monarch since the time of ancient Rome to make a concerted effort to bring together all the arts as a way of impressing his power both on his subjects and on visiting foreign dignitaries. He wanted, moreover, to use art as a way of expressing the greatness and glory of France itself.

In order to do so, Louis played an active role in French art. In 1648, he and the painter Charles Le Brun founded the Royal Academy of Painting and Sculpture. For the rest of Louis's reign, this organization—and its literary equivalent, the French Academy—dictated the French "national" style and supervised the images and messages that French artists presented in their work.

Central to the success of the project was the rigorous control of the way in which the king himself was presented in art. At the time, royal portraits were

often the only way in which subjects came into contact with their ruler, so monarchs had long been careful to project an impression of power and wealth. Louis was the foremost of a new series of absolute monarchs, or rulers in whom all the powers of the state were invested. Louis XIV famously said: "*L'État c'est moi*" ("I am the State"). He presented himself to the world as the Sun King, a version of the Greek sun god Apollo, who shone upon everything and saw everything, and whom the Greeks thought of as the creator of the arts.

When the Italian sculptor and architect Gianlorenzo Bernini visited Paris in 1665, Louis commissioned him to make a portrait bust of him. Contemporaries admired the bust for its realism, but it also made clear and flattering allusion to ancient busts of Alexander the Great. Perhaps, too, Louis wanted to draw a parallel between his own and Alexander's ideas about kingship.

Architecture was another important way in which Louis expressed the power and wealth of France. Louis's chief minister Jean-Baptiste Colbert (1619–1683) told the king: "Your majesty knows that apart from impressive achievements in war, nothing is so well able to show the greatness and spirit of princes than buildings." In 1669, Louis ordered work to begin on the Palace of Versailles, with which he intended to dazzle his subjects and the whole of Europe. It took over a half-century and sev-

eral generations of architects, designers, and artisans to complete what many consider to be the final masterpiece of the Baroque. Louis personally oversaw almost every detail, and every detail told the same story, that Louis XIV was the greatest ruler the world had ever known. Inside, the palace decorations and sculptures commemorated the king's achievements on the battlefield and in diplomacy. Outside, in a vast park designed by the landscape designer André Le Nôtre (1613–1700), a dramatic fountain sculpture continued the theme of Louis as the sun god Apollo, riding his chariot at dawn from its night-time resting place under the sea.

This modern photograph shows the sun god Apollo rising from the waters of a fountain in the gardens of Versailles.

The Palace of Versailles was the wonder and envy of the whole of Europe. Every detail, from the sculptures in its huge park to the paintings in the sumptuous state rooms, was designed to bear witness to the glory of France and Louis XIV.

feminist slant to the seduction scenes common in Dutch art of this period by showing women resisting the advances of their suitors, rather than giving in to them.

Art and the Scientific Revolution

This art of the everyday is sometimes linked to the same intellectual currents that produced the Scientific Revolution (*see 2:265*). The painstaking observation of the real world found in Dutch art has a parallel in the empirical, or observational, methods developed by such a scientist and thinker as the Frenchman René Descartes. Sometimes, too, artists exploited scientific tools, such as in their use of the camera obscura.

The earliest versions of the camera obscura, whose name derives from the Latin for "dark chamber," were used for viewing solar eclipses safely. The device consisted of a darkened room, or box, into which light was admitted by a tiny hole. The result was an inverted, or upside-down and reversed, image of the eclipse or outside scene on the wall opposite the hole. By the sixteenth century, artists were using lens-enhanced versions of the camera obscura to achieve perspective effects in their work.

One of the greatest seventeenth-century Dutch artists, Jan Vermeer (1632–1675), almost certainly used the camera obscura. Some scholars point out that the sparkling luminosity of his work parallels the effects created by the primitive lenses of the period. However, while Vermeer may indeed have anchored his art in such mechanical techniques, his paintings are filled with a sensuous Baroque poetry. He transforms reality by bathing his pictures in a rich light, achieving a subtle harmony of color and form.

The Art of the Individual

In his work, Vermeer often concentrates on an individual caught unawares in a private moment, such as a woman reading a letter or a girl intent on her sewing. In this respect, Vermeer's art reflects the seventeenth century's heightened awareness of individual experience or subjectivity.

Something similar can be found in the work of the Dutch Calvinist artist Rembrandt Harmensz van Rijn (1609–1669), who more than any artist before him made his own image the subject of his art. More than a hundred surviving paintings and etchings show the artist at every stage of his life, from impetuous youth to confident middle-aged citizen to troubled old man. Rembrandt's art is profoundly Protestant in spirit, setting the ordinary, questioning individual firmly at center stage.

This self-portrait of about 1660 belongs to the last decade of Rembrandt's life. The artist is almost brutal in the honesty with which he portrays the effects of age and self-doubt.

In this seventeenth-century camera obscura, a pinhole aperture projected an image onto the back of the box.

A seventeenth-century print entitled *The Harmony of the Universe* shows the Earth at the center of the universe, surrounded by a series of perfect spheres. This system, proposed by Ptolemy in the second century, formed the basis of astronomy for 1,300 years.

The Scientific Revolution

A Changing Understanding of the World

The late sixteenth and seventeenth centuries saw great changes in how people understood the universe. People began to try to understand the world, not in terms of religion, but in terms of what they could see and deduce. The name often given to this change, the scientific revolution, implies that the process was sudden. In fact, it took place over a period of two and a half centuries. Neither was the process a smooth development from ignorance to knowledge. It involved the work of many people, who each made their own contribution. There were many false starts, wrong turns, and dead ends.

Science and Religion

To Europeans of the mid-sixteenth century, the universe was a sacred place, governed by God's will. At its center was the Earth, home to God's most important creation, humankind. The discoveries of the scientific revolution would chip away at such certainties and challenge some of the fundamental beliefs of Christianity.

The people at the forefront of the scientific revolution, however, did not set out to replace religion with science. On the contrary, they believed that, by discovering the secrets of nature, they enhanced rather than reduced God's glory. Church leaders did not always agree. Both Catholics and Protestants persecuted scientific pioneers for their beliefs.

Those pioneers were not like modern scientists; it is more accurate to call them natural philosophers. They saw nature as a book in which they could read the meaning of creation. They often pursued a wide range of studies—religion, philosophy, mathematics, physics, astronomy, and law—to help interpret the natural world. They even studied fields that today we do not think of as scientific, such as magic, alchemy, and astrology.

Traditional Assumptions

Many assumptions about the world drew on the work of ancient Greek and Roman authors. Over the centuries, their theories had become closely linked with the teachings of the Bible to create the Christian view of nature. The second-century Greek astronomer Ptolemy placed Earth at the center of the universe. Even earlier, the Greek philosopher Aristotle explained that all matter comprises four elements—fire, water, air, and earth—and a combination of four qualities: heat, cold, dryness, and humidity. Aristotle also proposed that nothing moved unless it was made to by some force. The Earth could not be moving, the theory implied, because there was no force big enough to move it. Alternative expla-

A 1482 illustration shows Ptolemy holding an armillary sphere, a model of the universe. As well as being an outstanding astronomer, the ancient Greek also studied geography and produced detailed maps of Asia and large parts of Africa.

266

nations of motion could be more fanciful. A stone falling to the ground speeded up because it was happy to be going home.

The human body was equally misunderstood. The balance of four "humors"—blood, phlegm, black bile, and yellow bile—determined a person's health. Doctors followed the teachings of the Roman physician Galen. By dissecting animals, Galen concluded that there were two separate blood systems in the body, one bluish and one red, and that blood came from the liver.

Conditions for Change

By the mid-sixteenth century, such traditional beliefs were under threat. The cultural reawakening of the Renaissance (*see 1:79*) had stirred up intellectual ferment and encouraged a questioning of the works of classical authorities. Meanwhile, the Reformation broke the Catholic Church's monopoly over spiritual matters, creating an atmosphere in which new ideas had a better chance of developing. The exploration of the New World stimulated Europeans to expand their horizons. Social and economic changes disrupted old patterns of behavior, creating new opportunities. The invention of printing helped new ideas circulate widely and rapidly.

Even so, people resisted change. Vesalius (1514–1564), a Belgian anatomist, found two hundred errors in Galen's works. Galen, for example, said that the human thigh bone is curved, like a dog's. Even when Vesalius proved that the thigh bone is straight, some Galenists blamed the fact on the contemporary fashion for tight trousers!

Nicolaus Copernicus (1473–1543)

The scientific revolution began in astronomy, one of the oldest branches of science. The movement of the heavens dictated the calendar by which people lived. Ancient peoples, such as the Maya of Central America, made careful records of the stars and planets. Now, as their voyages grew longer, sailors needed better astronomical observations to help with navigation.

In 1514, the Catholic Church asked the Polish astronomer Nicolaus Copernicus for advice on reforming the calendar.

A wooden astrolabe from the time of Copernicus, with movable bands to show the orbits of the planets. Only six of the nine planets were known: Earth, Mars, Mercury, Venus, Jupiter, and Saturn.

Because of an error in calculation, the calendar and the astronomical movements it recorded no longer matched. Copernicus set out to gain better information on the movement of the Sun and Moon. He realized that the problems with the calendar were not only the result of inaccurate data. They also arose from people's model of the solar system.

That model takes its name from its inventor, the Greek Ptolemy. The Ptolemaic

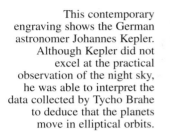

This contemporary engraving shows the German astronomer Johannes Kepler. Although Kepler did not excel at the practical observation of the night sky, he was able to interpret the data collected by Tycho Brahe to deduce that the planets move in elliptical orbits.

The Danish astronomer Tycho Brahe, shown in a contemporary engraving, produced detailed observations that helped to refine the work of Nicolaus Copernicus.

system placed Earth at the center of the universe. The planets, Sun, and stars revolved around it on glasslike spheres that moved in circles that reflected the perfection of God's creation. Ptolemy's geocentric, or Earth-centered, model survived for 1,300 years. It fitted well with the Christian view of God placing his human creation at the center of the universe.

The Ptolemaic system did not, however, fit with what astronomers actually saw. Ever more accurate astronomical observations showed up faults in Ptolemy's system. To explain them, mathematicians developed an increasingly complex model of the solar system. One Spanish patron of the sciences complained: "If the Almighty had consulted me before the Creation, I should have recommended something simpler."

A New View
Copernicus proposed an alternative heliocentric, or Sun-centered, model of the solar system, in which Earth orbited the Sun and also rotated daily on its own axis. Copernicus was afraid to publish his theory, however. Only in 1540 did one of Copernicus's pupils take the manuscript of the astronomer's *On the Revolutions of the Celestial Spheres* to the printer. Leaders of the Protestant Reformation prevented the book from being printed in Germany, so publication was further delayed. Copernicus is said to have received the first copy on the day he died, in May 1543.

The Legacy of Copernicus
Copernicus himself was uneasy with the implications of his work. How could his research be reconciled with the Bible, which placed a motionless Earth at the center of the universe? How could common sense believe that the Earth was racing through space at tremendous speed, when it did not feel as though it was moving? Copernicus himself seems to have got cold feet. He claimed in the book's introduction, written just before publication, that its findings were hypothetical.

Copernicus's theory implied that the universe was far larger than anyone imagined. If he was right, then the stars would slightly change their patterns each month. If those changes could not be seen from Earth, then it must be because the stars were very far away. At the same time, if Earth was not the center of the universe, then why did objects fall to the ground when they were dropped? Above all, if Earth were not the center of the universe, then how could humankind believe that the universe existed only for its benefit?

This contemporary engraving shows Stellaborg, the observatory Tycho Brahe built in a castle on an island off the coast of Denmark. Brahe's wealth allowed him to furnish the observatory with the best equipment available in Europe.

Escaping the Hold of Tradition

Eventually, Copernicus's heliocentric system posed almost as many problems for mathematicians as the Ptolemaic model of the universe. Copernicus had retained from Ptolemy the mistaken idea that celestial bodies moved in perfect circles. Copernicus was not alone in only partly rejecting the Ptolemaic theory. The great Italian astronomer Galileo also believed that planetary orbits were circular. It was hard for scientists to escape the idea of circular orbits. They were part of a larger commitment to the Christian notion that the heavens were perfect and eternal.

Tycho and Kepler

There was growing proof that planetary orbits were not circular. The astronomer Tycho Brahe (1546–1601), an eccentric Danish noble with a false nose made of silver—he lost most of his own nose in a

Galileo Galilei, the Italian mathematician and astronomer, shown at the height of his career in a colored drawing by Ottavio Leoni. 269

duel over mathematics—made a detailed set of astronomical observations without even a telescope. He also observed the path of a comet, which disproved the theory that the planets moved on glasslike spheres. The comet would have crashed through them. After Tycho's death in 1601, his assistant, the German Johannes Kepler (1571–1630), used the observations to compile a set of tables showing that the planets moved in ellipses, rather than circles.

Tycho's observations also allowed him to calculate the true length of the year to within less than a second. In 1582, Pope Gregory XIII dropped ten days from the year to bring the calendar and the heavens back into harmony.

The Contribution of Galileo

Galileo Galilei (1564–1642) was one of the outstanding figures of the scientific revolution. His career demonstrates the importance of patronage. Scholars relied on patrons to fund experiments. Galileo won the backing of the Medici family, rulers of the city of Florence, by improving the telescope, which he made thirty times more powerful than before, and the compass. Both devices had military and economic applications. Patrons of science wanted practical benefit for their investment.

Much of Galileo's work revolved around proving that Copernicus had been correct. With his improved telescope, he made many astronomical discoveries including the phases of Venus, Jupiter's planets, and the nature of Sun spots. The heavens were by no means as unchanging as people had believed. Galileo also overcame the commonsense objection to Copernicus that Earth does not feel as if it is moving. Galileo's argument was that all motion is relative. Just as the cargo on a ship does not move relative to the ship itself, only to the shore, so objects on the Earth share the same motion and do not move relative to each other.

Facing the Inquisition

Galileo's work brought him into conflict with the Catholic Church, which remained strong in Italy. The church believed that the Bible made sense only if Earth stood at the center of the universe. For arguing the opposite, Galileo stood trial for heresy. A court of the Inquisition in Rome forced him

to withdraw his belief that Earth orbits the Sun. Even as the defeated astronomer left the court, it is said that he muttered, "Yet it does move." Galileo spent the last eight years of his life under house arrest in the Italian countryside, where he continued observe the night sky until his sight failed near the end of his life.

Galileo's clash with the church was not a simple battle between religion and science. Supporters of both sides claimed to be just as devout Catholics as their opponents. While the church maintained that the Bible should be interpreted literally on all subjects, Galileo objected that its purpose was not to teach people astronomy. He claimed that the Bible teaches "how to go to Heaven, not how the heavens go."

Sir Francis Bacon

Developments in astronomy had parallels in all fields of thought, as people began to apply a reasoned approach to the world. The Englishman Sir Francis Bacon (1561–

One of the telescopes Galileo built to assist in his observations of the heavens. Galileo's telescopes were more powerful than any yet seen, thanks largely to the skilled grinding of glass lenses for magnification.

1626), for example, is famous not for any discovery but for his insights into how science should be conducted.

Bacon believed in the importance of establishing facts before proceeding to conclusions. Those facts had to be empirical, or measurable and objective, rather than dependent on personal perception. In an ideal world, the facts would be gathered by the "House of Solomon," named for the wise ruler of the Bible. The members of the institution would have different roles. Some would travel to gather information. Some would study old books. Some would carry out experiments. Others would organize the results into tables or work on possible technical applications of the findings. Finally, those whom Bacon called "interpreters of nature" would organize the findings into theories.

This division of labor would ensure that theories about the natural world developed from real evidence, not personal prejudice. Humans would achieve a "knowledge of all causes, and secret motions of things." Shortly afterward, Bacon believed, Christ would return to Earth. Like his contemporaries, Bacon did not see his emphasis on the scientific and rational as a challenge to Christianity, but as a complement to it.

René Descartes (1596–1650)

In France, the philosopher René Descartes was developing his own view of the world. Descartes spent his early life fighting as a soldier in the Thirty Years' War (*see 2:225*). As he moved from place to place, he became convinced that humans knew very few absolute truths about the world. People held to traditional assumptions about the world with no proof that they were true. Customs and philosophies varied so much that none could claim to be true. The human senses seemed an unreliable way to seek absolute truths. How something looked or felt varied from person to person and even within the same person, depending upon the individual's condition, health, or age.

How was it possible to know anything for sure? Descartes returned to basic principles. He began by disbelieving everything that it was possible to doubt and concluded that the only thing he could not doubt was that he was actually doubting. If he was doubting, however, then he must exist. He expressed his conclusion in his famous phrase, "I think, therefore I am."

The Mechanistic World

The conclusion "I think, therefore I am" proved to Descartes that his mind existed, even if it could not be explained. He could

understand the physical world, however, through geometry, the science of shapes. All matter could be described by geometric rules. There was no such thing as a vacuum. Even apparently empty space was filled with invisible particles of matter. These impacted on one another to cause all motion, from leaves flying in the wind to the planets orbiting the Sun. All movement was the result of the interaction of matter upon matter.

At the core of Descartes's understanding of natural phenomena lies the idea that nature functions like a complicated, interlocking machine, a clockwork mechanism in which each element has an effect on others. Descartes's view—called a mechanistic view—was at odds with the emphasis Catholic theology placed on God's intervention in the universe. The philosopher found it easier to work in Protestant Holland than in his native France.

Sir Isaac Newton

The scientific revolution reached its culmination in the work of the Englishman Isaac Newton (1642–1727). Experts recog-

This manor house in Tuscany is where Galileo spent the last years of his life under house arrest. The astronomer continued to observe the heavens until he went blind, when he complained that, while he had enlarged the universe for everyone else, his own world had shrunk to nothing.

271

nize Newton as one of the greatest scientists ever and credit him with completing the triumph of the mechanistic worldview. Newton discovered the basic laws that govern the movement of matter in the universe, a problem that had puzzled thinkers for centuries. His most famous discovery was that of gravity, the force that draws bodies toward other bodies. Legend has it that he began to consider the problem after seeing an apple fall from a tree. In optics, Newton discovered that light is made up of a spectrum of colors. In mathematics, he formulated calculus, a complex calculation system still used in a variant form today.

Newton was an ambitious man. He feuded with other scientists, often because he claimed credit for others' work. In contrast to Galileo, placed under house arrest, Newton enjoyed great prestige. In 1703, he became president of the Royal Society, a body set up to encourage scientific research. In 1705, he was knighted. On his death in 1727, he received a state funeral.

The Spiritual Mechanist

Newton's laws of motion explained much of the universe in mechanical terms. For the scientist himself, however, the world was as spiritual as it had been for sixteenth-century scientists. He spent as much time studying theology and alchemy as physics. One of his preoccupations was trying to calculate the date of Christ's second coming from clues in the Book of Revelations.

For Newton, the law that described the effects of gravity, for example, still did not explain what gravity was. That question remained one of God's mysteries. Newton described the limitations of his own achievements: "To myself, I seem to have been only like a boy playing on the sea-

A painting of the French philosopher René Descartes by Frans Hals, from about 1640. Descartes believed it was necessary to disbelieve everything in science that could not be proved with scientific or philosophic evidence.

A contemporary portrait of Isaac Newton, of whom the poet Alexander Pope wrote: "God said let Newton be / And all was light."

shore, and diverting myself in now and then finding a smoother pebble or prettier shell than ordinary, whilst the great ocean of truth lay all undiscovered before me."

Newton brought the scientific revolution to its peak by synthesizing the knowledge of men such as Copernicus and Galileo. He said, "If I have seen further than other men, it is because I have stood on the shoulders of giants." Newton's discoveries were the basis for much scientific research after his death. His influence went beyond science, inspiring social and political philosophers to see their subjects in mechanistic terms. Newton ushered in the Age of Reason, when people assumed that science could explain everything about the universe.

A Scientific Approach

The scientific revolution had established experimentation, measurement, and deduction as the fundamental principles of investigating the world. They were tools useful in a range of subjects: the compilation of tide tables, the discoveries of Earth's magnetic field, and the circulation of blood. The voyages of discovery, meanwhile, revealed a world of greater variety than ever imagined, full of new plants and animals to be described and classified. Microscopes

The first reflecting telescope, built by Isaac Newton in 1668, used mirrors inside the telescope's barrel to achieve higher magnification than earlier devices could manage.

273

revealed for the first time the tiny organisms that we now know cause disease.

As the scientific approach became more general, superstition weakened in western Europe. After 1640, for example, witch trials virtually died out (*see 2:182*). The scientific approach took longer to become established in some countries than others. Even on the Italian peninsula, however, the dominance of the Catholic Church did not prevent Enlightenment thought from flourishing in the cities of Naples, Florence, and Milan.

Academies of Science

The mid-seventeenth century saw the founding of two great academies that enshrined the empirical approach, the Royal Society of London and the Académie des Sciences of Paris. They published scientific papers, making discoveries public. For a theory to be accepted, it had to be tested and verified by a scientist's contemporaries. During the scientific revolution, individuals had advanced knowledge piecemeal. The academies would be the powerhouses for more systematic advances in the future.

A color engraving shows Isaac Newton observing rays of light in a darkened room. Newton's scientific breakthroughs were often made with simple equipment and experiments.

Time Line

	EUROPE POLITICAL HISTORY	EUROPE CULTURAL HISTORY	EVENTS IN THE REST OF THE WORLD
1400	**1415** In Bohemia, Jan Hus is burned at the stake for heresy		
			1444 200 African slaves arrive in Portugal, beginning large-scale European involvement in the slave trade
1450	**1452** The Habsburg Frederick III is crowned Holy Roman emperor	**1450** German printer Johannes Gutenberg invents movable metal type, which revolutionizes printing	
		1455 The Gutenberg Bible is published in Germany. From this time on, printing with movable type means that more books and pamphlets are available to ordinary people.	**1453** Muslim forces capture Constantinople, capital of Orthodox Christianity
1460			
1470	**1473** Marriage of Ferdinand and Isabella unites Aragon and Castile		
	1477 Frederick III extends his empire by marrying his son Maximilian to the daughter of the duke of Burgundy	**1477** William Caxton starts printing books and pamphlets in English language	
	1478 The Council of the Spanish Church institutes major reforms in the Church in Spain		
1480			
	1483 Tomás de Torquemada establishes Supreme Council of the Inquisition		
	1485 In England Henry Tudor defeats Richard III at Battle of Bosworth. As Henry VII he becomes the first Tudor monarch of the Tudor dynasty.	**1486** *The Hammer of Witches* is published in Rome	
1490			**1492** Christopher Columbus makes landfall in the Bahamas
	1493 Frederick III dies and his son Maximilian succeeds him as Holy Roman emperor. Maximilian marries his son Philip to the daughter of Ferdinand and Isabella.		

15th Century	16th Century	17th Century

EUROPE POLITICAL HISTORY	EUROPE CULTURAL HISTORY	EVENTS IN THE REST OF THE WORLD
	c. 1500 Around the beginning of the sixteenth century landowners start switching from crops to sheep, in response to the increased demand for cloth.	**c. 1500** Cod from Newfoundland becomes an important addition to the European diet
1501 Isma'il becomes shah of Iran, beginning reign of Safavid dynasty
1509 Henry VIII of England succeeds to the throne at the age of eighteen		**1510** The Portuguese establish a trading base at Goa, India
c. 1510 First African slaves shipped to Caribbean
	1511 The Dutchman Desiderius Erasmus publishes *Praise of Folly,* in which he criticizes materialism and hypocrisy	**1514** Turkish Ottoman army defeats the Safavids at the Battle of Chaldiran
1517 Martin Luther nails his Ninety-Five Theses to the door of a church in Wittenberg, protesting against abuses in the Catholic Church		**1517** Portuguese traders reach China
1519 The Habsburg Charles I of Spain is named as Holy Roman emperor		
1520 Charles I of Spain is crowned as Charles V, emperor elect. Pope Leo X excommunicates Martin Luther for heresy.	**1520 and following** The rise in population in Europe makes it increasingly difficult for agriculture to feed everybody. Food prices rise dramatically, and peasants start leaving the land to find work in the cities.	**1520** Magellan rounds the tip of South American and sails across the Pacific
1521–1523 The emperor Charles V seizes Tournai and Milan from the French	**1522** Martin Luther starts translating the Bible into German	**1521** Spanish conquistador Hernán Cortés overthrows the Aztec empire
		1523 Spain creates Council of Indies to administer colonies in the New World
1524 At Battle of Pavia, Charles V's army defeats the French. In southern Germany the Peasants' Revolt demands the abolition of serfdom.	**c. 1525** Lutheran services in the German Protestant principalities are conducted in German rather than Latin	
1526 League of Cognac unites the pope, England, France, and several Italian cities against the Holy Roman emperor Charles V	**1526** The New Testament is translated into English from Greek	**1526** Mogul emperor Babur founds Mogul empire in India
1527 Charles V's Habsburg army sacks Rome and puts the pope to flight		
1529 Treaty of Combrai signed, making peace between the emperor Charles V and France		
1531 The German Protestant princes form the Schmalkaldic League to challenge Habsburg power in Germany	**1532** Lutheranism spreads to Scandinavia	**1532** Francisco Pizarro overcomes the Incas of Peru
1534 Henry VIII of England establishes the Church of England. The Treaty of Augsburg allies Francis I of France with the Protestant princes against Emperor Charles V.		**1535** French navigator Jacques Cartier sails up the Saint Lawrence River and claims Canada for the French
1536 Henry VIII of England dissolves the monasteries and seizes their assets	**1536** John Calvin publishes *Institutes of the Christian Religion*	

15th Century	16th Century	17th Century

EUROPE POLITICAL HISTORY	EUROPE CULTURAL HISTORY	EVENTS IN THE REST OF THE WORLD
1540 Hostilities break out again between Emperor Charles V and France **1541** Calvin is invited to Geneva to set up a reformed church there **1542** Pope Paul III sets up the Roman Inquistion **1544** The emperor Charles V joins with Henry VIII of England in an invasion of France. Truce of Crespy between the emperor Charles V and France. **1545** The Council of Trent is convened by Pope Paul III **1547** Charles V crushes the Schmalkaldic League at Battle of Mühlberg. Francis I of France and Henry VIII of England die. **1552** In the Treaty of Chambord, Henry II of France promises support to the Protestant princes in Germany **1555** The Peace of Augsburg grants freedom to the German Protestant princes to introduce Lutherism in their own territories **1556** The emperor Charles V abdicates, handing over the imperial title to his brother Ferdinand and the Spanish crown to his son Philip **1558** Mary, queen of England, dies and her half sister becomes Elizabeth I of England **1559** Philip II of Spain makes peace with France in the Treaty of Cateau-Cambresis; Henry II is succeeded by Francis II of France. **1562** Catholics massacre Huguenots in the French town of Vassy. Huguenots rise throughout France under the prince of Condé, starting years of civil war. **1566** Calvinists in the Netherlands storm Catholic churches and destroy sacred images **1567** Philip II of Spain sends the Duke of Alba to the Netherlands to crush the Calvinist revolt **1568** William of Orange invades the Netherlands but is defeated by the Spanish	**1540** Spanish discover silver at Potosí, Bolivia **1543** Nicolaus Copernicus publishes *On the Revolution of the Heavenly Spheres*, in which he proposes the radical idea that the sun is the center of the universe, and the Earth revolves around it **c. 1550** The Low Countries (present-day Holland and Belgium) become the richest region in Europe, due to their trading activities **1553** A violent persecution of Protestants starts in England, under the new Catholic queen, Mary I **1558** In England, the Elizabethan Age begins, in which poets, playwrights, and musicians flourish. Church services are conducted in English rather than Latin. **1560** Over the next ten years Calvinism spreads to Scotland and southern France	**1556** Akbar ascends the throne of India. Under Akbar, arts and architecture flourish. Delhi and Lahore are among the world's biggest cities.

15th Century	16th Century	17th Century

	EUROPE POLITICAL HISTORY	EUROPE CULTURAL HISTORY	EVENTS IN THE REST OF THE WORLD
1570—	**1570** The Peace of Saint-Germain allows French Huguenots to worship freely in the countryside. At the Battle of Lepanto, Spanish and Venetian forces defeat the Turks. **1572** The St. Bartholomew's Day Massacre, in which two to three thousand Protestants are massacred in Paris **1572–1576** Netherland cities rebel against Spanish rule	**1574** The French Protestant reformer Theodore Beza publishes *On the Right of Magistrates over Their Subjects*, which maintains that subjects are not bound to obey a king who has offended against God	**1576** Death of Shah Tahmasp begins a decade of civil war in Iran
1580—	 **1584** The Catholic League is formed in France under Henry, duke of Guise, to fight the Protestants **1585–1589** King Henry III, Henry of Navarre, and Henry of Guise struggle for control of France in the so-called War of the Three Henries	**1585** The Flemish mathematician Simon Stevin invents the decimal system for calculations, replacing the old system of counting in twelves	**1580** Philip II of Spain annexes Portugal, adding Portugal's overseas possessions to the Spanish empire **1584** Sir Walter Raleigh explores the east coast of North America, which he names Virginia
	1588 Philip II of Spain sends his armada to invade England, but it is defeated and scattered **1589** Henry III of France, the last of the Valois kings, is stabbed to death by a fanatical friar		**1588** Shah Abbas I comes to power in Iran
1590—	**1593** Henry IV of France (formerly Henry of Navarre) reconverts to Catholicism to secure his crown **1598** The Edict of Nantes ends the religious wars in France and grants French Protestants freedom of worship within their own homes		
1600—		**1600** By the end of the fifteenth century about half the male population of European cities can read and write	**1600** English East India Company is formed **1602** Dutch East India Company is formed to trade with the East Indies
	1603 James VI of Scotland succeeds to the English throne as James I **1605** In England, a Catholic plot led by Guy Fawkes tries to blow up the houses of Parliament		**1606** English merchants receive royal charter to set up a colony in Virginia
	1609 A truce is agreed between the Netherlands and Spain	**1609** A modern banking system is founded in Amsterdam. Trade in the Netherlands is the basis for a wealthy merchant class.	

15th Century	16th Century	17th Century

278

EUROPE POLITICAL HISTORY	EUROPE CULTURAL HISTORY	EVENTS IN THE REST OF THE WORLD

1610 —

1618 The Defenestration of Prague starts the Thirty Years' War

1619 Frederick V of the Palatinate is crowned king of Bohemia

1620 —
1620 Battle of the White Mountain near Prague, in which the forces of the Catholic League defeat Frederick of Bohemia, thereby crushing the Bohemian revolt

1625 Charles I succeeds to the throne of England

1628 The English Parliament forces Charles I to accept the Petition of Right

1629 The emperor Ferdinand II bans the practice of Calvinism in Germany. Charles I of England dissolves Parliament.

1630 —
1630 Gustavus Adolphus of Sweden enters the Thirty Years' War, landing in Germany to prevent further loss of Protestant lands

1631 In the Battle of Breitenfeld, Swedish forces defeat the imperial army

1634 At the Battle of Nördlingen imperial and Spanish forces defeat the Swedes and Germans.

1635 The Peace of Prague offers an amnesty to most of the Protestant princes involved in the Thirty Years' War; France declares war on Spain

1640 —
1640 Charles I of England recalls Parliament, but it refuses to vote him any money and he dismisses it after three weeks. Charles I of England convenes the Long Parliament.

1641 In England, Parliament executes the Earl of Stafford, Charles I's chief supporter and adviser

1642 Charles I of England declares war on Parliament, starting the English civil war

1645 The English Parliament forms the New Model Army, commanded by Thomas Fairfax. The English Parliamentary forces defeat the Royalists at the Battle of Naseby.

1611 James I of England commissions an English translation of the Bible, the "King James Version"

1613 In Italy the astronomer Galileo Galilei uses powerful telescopes to study the heavens, confirming that Copernicus was right in claiming that the Earth revolves around the sun.

1616 Galileo is arrested by the Inquisition for heresy

1630 During the Thirty Years' War, much of the German countryside is devastated, leaving houses and farms in ruins

1644 The French philosopher René Descartes publishes his *Principles of Philosophy* in which he sets out his mechanistic view of the world, maintaining that all physical phenomena are interconnected like a clockwork mechanism

---

c. 1630 A great migration begins of English Puritans to North America

1631 Famine sweeps India

15th Century	16th Century	17th Century

EUROPE POLITICAL HISTORY	EUROPE CULTURAL HISTORY	EVENTS IN THE REST OF THE WORLD
1648 The Peace of Westphalia grants independence to the Dutch republic and increased independence to the German princes **1649** Charles I of England is executed as a traitor	**c. 1650** In the mid–seventeenth century, the Dutch painters Rembrandt and Vermeer produce pictures depicting ordinary life for private wealthy patrons	
1653 In England the New Model Army dismisses Parliament and appoints Oliver Cromwell as Lord Protector	**1653** Under the Commonwealth, English society becomes increasingly puritan. Music, theaters, dancing, and gambling are discouraged or forbidden. Bible reading, praying, and fasting take their place.	**1652** Dutch settlers establish Cape Town at the southern tip of Africa as a staging post for ships sailing to the Far East
	1657 The pendulum clock is invented by Christiaan Huygens, a Dutch physicist	**1658** Alamgir succeeds to the Mogul throne in India
1660 The English Restoration. After the death of Oliver Cromwell a new Parliament invites Charles II to return as king.	**1660** In London, England, the writer Samuel Pepys begins keeping his *Diary*	
	1665 In England, the Great Plague kills 75,000 Londoners **1666** The Great Fire rages through London, destroying four-fifths of the city **1667** The English poet John Milton—formerly secretary to Oliver Cromwell—publishes his epic poem *Paradise Lost*	
	1671 Antonie van Leewenhoek constructs the first microscope and later uses it to detect tiny organisms such as bacteria that are invisible to the naked eye	
		1680–1700 Witch crazes sweep North America. In 1692, nineteen witches are killed at Salem, Massachusetts.
1685 James II succeeds his brother as king of England	**1682** Louis XIV of France takes up residence in his new palace at Versailles, designed to be a wonder of the world and a testament to the power and wealth of France	
1688 William of Orange lands in England. James II escapes to France. **1689** William of Orange and his wife Mary (James II's daughter) are crowned jointly as William and Mary of England	**1687** The English mathematician Isaac Newton publishes his *Mathematical Principles of Natural Philosophy,* which sets out the law of universal gravitation	

Timeline markers (left): 1650, 1660, 1670, 1680

15th Century	16th Century	17th Century

Glossary

absolution In the Catholic Church, the forgiveness of sins, made by a priest on behalf of Christ.

alchemy A form of chemistry that originated in Alexandria about 100 B.C.E. and was still practiced in the Middle Ages. Alchemy aimed to find the elixir of life—a medicinal preparation that would prolong life—and a way of turning metals into gold.

apprentice somebody legally bound for a number of years to a master craftsman in order to learn a trade. The apprentice system originated in England in the fourteenth century and was the acccepted way of training new recruits into the craft guilds.

armada a Spanish word meaning "an armed force." In particular, armada was the name given to the fleet of 130 warships sent by Philip II of Spain to invade England in 1588. The Spanish ships were attacked by the English navy and put to flight.

astrolabe a navigational aid used for measuring the altitude of the sun or stars. It was widely used by mariners in the fifteenth and sixteenth centuries until superseded by the sextant.

auto-da-fé a Spanish term meaning "act of faith." Auto-da-fé referred to the ceremony of the passing of judgment by a court of the Inquisition and the carrying out of the sentence. Those found guilty of heresy were generally burnt at the stake.

baroque a style of art and architecture that evolved in Europe in the seventeenth century. It was characterized by rich colors and ornate, flowing lines.

body politic a traditional concept of social organization in which each person had an allotted role to perform. The idea of the body politic began to break down in the fifteenth century.

bureaucracy a form of government characterized by specialized administrators and hierarchies of officials.

camera obscura a Latin term meaning dark room that described a device artists used to project an image. The camera obscura was a lightproof box with a small hole in one side. An image of an outside scene or object was projected through the hole onto the opposite wall of the box, enabling artists to see perspective in a scene or to trace an image.

cardinal a high-ranking priest in the Catholic Church. A cardinal ranks immediately below the pope, who appoints a college of cardinals to assist him. There are about seventy cardinals at any one time, and it is they who elect a new pope.

chiaroscuro a Latin term meaning "light and dark" that describes a technique used in baroque painting of using intense contrasts between light areas and shade to increase dramatic effect.

Church of England the reformed church established in England during the sixteenth century with the English monarch as its head.

commonwealth a type of government in which power is exercised for the good of all a state's people. England was declared a commonwealth after the execution of Charles I in 1649.

crusades medieval military expeditions by European Christians to capture Palestine, or the Holy Land, from the Muslims.

diet a council or legislative body, most often the council or assembly of the constituent estates of the Holy Roman Empire. Diets are named for the towns or cities where they were held.

Diggers a radical group that appeared in England after the Civil War. They demanded the abolition of private property and the distribution of land to the people so that they could grow crops.

dissolution the name given to the destruction of monasteries and other religious foundations during the Reformation. In particular, the term refers to Henry VIII's seizure of the land and wealth of England's religious foundations between 1536 and 1540.

dynasty a succession of rulers who all come from the same family. Prominent dynasties in early modern Europe included the Habsburgs of Austria and Spain, the Valois of France, and the Tudors of England.

empirical a term describing knowledge gained by experience or observation, particularly from a scientific process of experiment, observation, and deduction. Empirical knowledge was a foundation of the scientific revolution of the sixteenth and seventeenth centuries.

enclosure the process of fencing off fields and common land for private use. Sixteenth-century European landowners enclosed land in order to keep sheep. The process often deprived villagers of land they used to raise crops or graze animals.

excommunication expulsion from the Roman Catholic Church, usually as a punishment for heresy.

feudal system a form of social organization, common in medieval Europe, that divided society into three estates: the nobility, the clergy, and everyone else. The estates were bound by a system of mutual duties and obligations. Lords provided protection for the peasants on their estates, for example; in return, peasants were tied to laboring in the service of the lord. The feudal system began to collapse in much of Europe in the early modern period.

guild a medieval craft association formed to protect its members, maintain standards, and regulate the training of apprentices. From around the twelfth century, guilds grew to be very powerful in many European towns.

heliocentric placing the sun rather than the Earth at the center of the universe. A heliocentric view of the solar system was proposed by Copernicus in the sixteenth century in opposition to the teaching of the Catholic Church.

heresy an opinion or belief that is contrary to the accepted doctrine, in particular of the Roman Catholic Church. In the fifteenth and sixteenth centuries, heresy was a serious crime and those found guilty of it were dealt with severely.

heretic someone, particularly a baptized Catholic, who held a view that was not acceptable to the Catholic Church.

Holy Roman Empire a central European empire of mainly Germanic states. The empire was ruled by an emperor elected by the most powerful German princes and had the pope as its spiritual head.

Huguenot the name given to French Protestants who mainly followed the Calvinist faith. The name Huguenot may have derived from an old German word for confederate or comrade.

indulgence in the Catholic Church, relief from all or part of the penance necessary to atone for sins. Indulgences were sometimes sold by the Roman Catholic Church to raise funds, a practice that led to vigorous objections by Martin Luther and other religious reformers.

inquisition the name for several different Catholic ecclesiastical courts set up to find and punish heretics. The chief inquisitions were the Roman Inquisition and the Spanish Inquisition.

Levellers a political group that arose in England during the Civil War. The Levellers wanted to declare a republic with equal rights for all citizens and religious tolerance.

mendicant a member of a religious order of friars or monks that forbids ownership of any kind of property. Mendicants had to exist on alms and begging.

monastery a building occupied by a community of monks who withdraw from the world to live according to rules of poverty and chastity, accompanied by regular praying and fasting.

Orthodox Christianity the main form of Christianity in Greece, Russia, and other parts of eastern Europe and western Asia. The Orthodox Church separated from Roman Catholicism because of longstanding differences in doctrine, especially concerning the authority of the pope.

Ottoman Empire a Muslim empire centered in Turkey that lasted from around 1300 to 1922. It was founded by the Ottoman Turks, a nomadic people from central Asia.

parliament a representative assembly of a nation's people that comes together to advise the ruler or to act as a lawmaking body. In most early modern countries, the parliament was dominated by the traditional nobility.

plague a fatal disease that appeared on numerous occasions in early modern Europe, killing great numbers of people. The disease, which was carried by fleas, caused fever, headache, sores, and enlarged glands in the groin and armpit. The Black Death, a particularly severe plague epidemic, killed between one-third and one-half of Europe's population in the fourteenth century.

Presbyterianism a Protestant movement in which churches are governed by a group of elders rather than by a minister or bishop.

privy council a body of close advisers appointed to help a monarch govern the country.

protector a term often used to describe a person put in charge of a kingdom if the legitimate monarch was a child. The title Lord Protector was also given to Oliver Cromwell during the time of the English Commonwealth.

Protestantism a major form of Christianity founded in western Europe in the sixteenth century, when many Christians separated from Catholicism.

Roman Catholicism a major world religion and the form of Christianity with the largest number of followers. The Roman Catholic Church, which is led by the pope from Rome, was western Europe's only form of Christianity until the Reformation of the early sixteenth century.

salvation in the Roman Catholic Church, the deliverance from the consequences of sin and the attainment of eternal bliss after death.

sanitation the provision for the disposal of sewage and solid waste. The lack of sanitation in the fifteenth and sixteenth centuries was a serious health risk.

schism a split or division into two opposed parties. The Great Schism in the Catholic Church occurred in 1378, when two opposing popes both claimed to be the spiritual head of the church: Urban VI in Rome and Clement VII in Avignon. The division remained until 1417 when Martin V was elected as sole pope.

Schmalkaldic League a league of eight German princes and eleven German cities formed in 1531 for the purpose of defending the Lutheran faith. The league was a response to the decree made by the Diet of Augsburg in 1530 that all Lutherans should recognize the supremacy of the pope.

scourge a lash or a whip used to inflict punishment.

scourging lashing or whipping as a punishment. Scourging, sometimes self inflicted, was a common punishment or penance in the Roman Catholic Church.

secular belonging to the civil rather than the church authorities.

strappado an instrument of torture by which a victim was bound and repeatedly raised above the ground and allowed to fall, wrenching his or her arms from their sockets. The strappado was used during the Inquisition.

venality a willingness to be bribed or otherwise corrupted. Religious reformers often accused the Catholic clergy of venality.

villein a peasant in the feudal system who was partly a slave and partly free. A villein was tied to his or her lord but in other respects he or she had the rights of a free person.

witch trial the trial of someone accused of being a witch. The accused at witch trials were usually women whose alleged crimes included black magic and worshiping the devil.

Further Resources

Religious Protest

Bainton, R. H. *The Reformation of the Sixteenth Century*. Boston, MA: Beacon Press, 1985.

———. *Age of the Reformation*. Melbourne, FL: Krieger Publishing Company, 1983.

Hillebrand, H., ed. *Protestant Reformation*. New York: HarperCollins, 1984.

Kittelson, J. M. *Luther the Reformer*. Minneapolis, MN: Augsburg Fortress Publications, 1987.

Lohse, B. *Martin Luther: An Introduction to his Life and Work*. Minneapolis, MN: Fortress Press, 1986.

Pettegree, A., ed. *The Early Reformation in Europe*. New York: Cambridge University Press, 1993.

Catholic Reform

Bossy, J. *Peace in the Post-Reformation*. New York: Cambridge University Press, 1998.

DeMolen, R. L., ed. *Religious Orders of the Catholic Reformation: In Honor of John C. Olin on His Seventy-Fifth Birthday*. New York: Fordham University Press, 1994.

Hsia, R. *The World of Catholic Renewal 1540–1770*. New York: Cambridge University Press, 1998.

Jones, M. *The Counter Reformation: Religion and Society in Early Modern Europe*. New York: Cambridge University Press, 1996.

Kidd, B. *The Counter Reformation 1550–1600*. Westport, CT: Greenwood Publishing Group, 1980.

Lindberg, C. *The European Reformations*. Malden, MA: Blackwell Publishing, 1996.

Mullett, M. *Counter Reformation*. New York: Routledge, 1984.

Olin, J., ed. *The Catholic Reformation: Savonarola to Ignatius Loyola*. New York: Fordham University Press, 1993.

O'Malley, J. *The First Jesuits*. Cambridge, MA: Harvard University Press, 1993.

Outram Evennett, H. *The Spirit of the Counter-Reformation*. Notre Dame, IN: University of Notre Dame Press, 1986.

Dissent and Control

Hansen, C. *Witchcraft at Salem*. New York: George Braziller, 1985.

Kamen, H. A. F. *The Spanish Inquisition: A Historical Revision*. New Haven, CT: Yale University Press, 1998.

Peters, E. *Inquisition*. Berkeley, CA: University of Calilfornia Press, 1989.

———, *Torture*. Philadelphia, PA: University of Pennsylvania Press, 1996.

Roth, C. *Spanish Inquisition*. London: W.W. Norton & Co., 1996.

Sharpe, J. *Instruments of Darkness: Witchcraft in Early Modern England*. Philadelphia, PA: University of Pennsylvania Press, 1997.

Spain and the Habsburg Empire

Berenger, J. and Simpson, C. A. *History of the Habsburg Empire 1273–1700*. Reading, MA: Addison Wesley Publishing Company, 1994.

Ingrao, C. W. *The Habsburg Monarchy, 1618–1815*. New York: Cambridge University Press, 1994.

———. *State and Society in Early Modern Austria*. West Lafayette, IN: Purdue University Press, 1994.

Kann, R. A. *A History of the Habsburg Empire 1526–1918*. Berkeley, CA: University of California Press, 1980.

Lovett, A. W. *Early Habsburg Spain, 1517–1598*. New York: Oxford University Press, 1986.

Mamatey, V. S. *Rise of the Habsburg Empire 1526–1815*. Melbourne, FL: Krieger Publishing Company, 1978.

The Wars of Religion

Hale, J. R. *War and Society in Renaissance Europe 1450–1620*. Montreal: McGill Queens University Press, 1998.

Holt, M. P. *The French Wars of Religion 1562–1629*. New York: Cambridge University Press, 1996.

Knecht, J. R. and Segun, M. *The French Wars of Religion 1559–1598*. Reading, MA: Addison Wesley Publishing Company, 1996.

Sproxton, J. *Violence and Religion: Attitudes Towards Militancy in the French Civil Wars and the English Revolution*. New York: Routledge, 1995.

Wood, J. B. *The King's Army: Warfare, Soldiers and Society During the Wars of Religion in France, 1562–1576*. New York: Cambridge University Press, 1996.

Tudor England

Doran, S. *England and Europe in the Sixteenth Century*. New York: St. Martin's Press, 1999.

Elton, G. R. *England Under the Tudors*. New York: Routledge, 1991.

Harrison, W. *The Description of England: The Classic Contemporary Account of Tudor Social Life*. Mineola, NY: Dover Publications, 1995.

Palliser, D. M. *The Age of Elizabeth: England Under the Later Tudors 1547–1603*. Reading, MA: Addison Wesley Publishing Company, 1992.

Weir, A. *Life of Elizabeth I*. New York: Ballantine Books, 1998

Williams, P. *The Later Tudors: England 1547–1603 (New Oxford History of England)* Oxford: Clarendon Press, 1995.

The Revolt of the Netherlands

Duke, A. *Reformation and Revolt in the Low Countries*. Rio Grande, OH: Hambledon Press, 1990.

Limm, P. *The Dutch Revolt, 1559–1648*. Reading, MA: Addison Wesley Publishing Company, 1995.

Schama, S. *The Embarrassment of Riches: An Interpretation of Dutch Culture in the Golden Age*. New York: Knopf, 1987.

Van Gelderen, M. *The Political Thought of the Dutch Revolt, 1555–1590*. New York: Cambridge University Press, 1993.

The Thirty Years' War

Asch, R. G. *The Thirty Years' War: The Holy Roman Empire and Europe, 1618–48*. New York: St. Martin's Press, 1997.

Limm, P. *The Thirty Years' War*. Reading, MA: Addison Wesley Publishing Company, 1984.

Parker, G. The Military Revolution. New York: Cambridge University Press, 1996.

Parker, G. & Adams, S., eds. *The Thirty Years' War*. London: Routledge Kegan & Paul, 1997.

Rabb, T. *The Thirty Years' War*. Lanham, MD: University Press of America, 1982.

England's Civil War

Ashley, M. P. *The English Civil War*. New York: St. Martin's Press, 1997.

Bennett, M. *The Civil Wars in Britain and Ireland, 1638–1651*. Malden, MA: Blackwell Publishing, 1996.

Carlin, N. *The Causes of the English Civil War*. Malden, MA: Blackwell Publishing, 1998.

Emberton, W. and Adair, J. *The English Civil War Day by Day*. Stroud, UK: Sutton Publishing, 1997.

Gaunt, P. *The British Wars, 1637–1651*. New York: Routledge, 1997.

Hill, C. *World Turned Upside Down: Radical Ideas During the English Revolution*. New York: Viking Press, 1991.

Hughes, A. *The Causes of the English Civil War*. New York: St. Martin's Press, 1999.

Kenyon, J.P., ed. *The Civil Wars: A Military History of England, Scotland & Ireland 1638–1660*. New York: Oxford University Press, 1998.

Everyday Life in Europe

Burt, R. *Enclosure Acts: Sexuality, Property, and Culture in Early Modern England*. Ithaca, NY: Cornell University Press, 1994.

Davis, N. Z. *Women on the Margins: Three Seventeenth Century Lives*. Stanford, CA: Stanford University Press, 1977.

Hill, C. *Liberty Against the Law: Some Seventeenth Century Controversies*. London: Allen Lane, 1996.

Mingay, G. *Parliamentary Enclosure in England: An Introduction to Its Causes, Incidence and Impact 1750–1850*. Reading, MA: Addison Wesley Publishing Company, 1998.

Neeson, J. M. *Commoners: Common Right, Enclosure and Social Change in England, 1700–1820*. New York: Cambridge University Press, 1996.

Slater, M. *Family Life in the Seventeenth Century: The Veneys of Claydon House*. New York: Routledge, Kegan & Paul, 1984.

The Baroque World

Baroque Painting. Hauppauge, NY: Barron's Educational Series, 1998.

Collaway, S. *Baroque Baroque: The Culture of Excess*. London: Phaidon Press Inc., 1994.

Finaldi, G. and Kitson, M. *Discovering the Italian Baroque: The Denis Mahon Collection*. New Haven, CT: Yale University Press, 1997.

Gruber, A., ed. *Classicism and the Baroque in Europe*. New York: Abbeville Press, 1996.

Sadie, J. A. *Companion to Baroque Music*. Berkeley, CA: University of California Press, 1998.

Summerson, J. N. *The Architecture of the Eighteenth Century*. New York: Thames and Hudson, 1986.

Toman, R., ed. *The Baroque*. Konemann, 1998.

The Scientific Revolution

Boorstin, D. J. *The Discoverers*. New York: Random House, 1983.

Fantoli, A. *Galileo: For Copernicanism and for the Church*. Notre Dame, IN: University of Notre Dame Press, 1996.

Koyre, A. *Astronomical Revolution: Copernicus–Kepler–Barelli*. Mineola, NY: Dover Publications, 1992.

Kuhn, T. S. *The Structure of Scientific Revolutions*. Chicago, IL: University of Chicago Press, 1996.

Newhouse, E. L., ed. *Inventors and Discoverers: Changing Our World*. Washington, D.C.: National Geographic Society, 1994.

Wright, R. *Scientific Romance*. London: Picador, 1999.

Illustration Credits

Index

Page numbers in *italic type* refer to illustrations and captions.

Page numbers in *italic type* refer to illustrations and captions.

Page numbers in *italic type* refer to illustrations and captions.